Crossing Bridges

What Biking Up the East Coast Taught Me About Life After 60

Lisa A. Watts

River House Press

© 2024 River House Press

All rights reserved. No part of this publication may be reproduced, stored in a retrieval system or transmitted in any form or by any means, electronic, mechanical, photocopying, recording or otherwise without the prior permision of the publisher or in accordance with the provisions of the Copyright, Designs and Patents Act 1988 or under the terms of any licence permitting limited copying issued by the Copyright Licensing Agency.

Published by River House Press, Barrington, RI USA

Cover design: Claudia Royston

Author photo: Michael McGuire

A CIP record for this book is available from the Library of Congress Cataloging-in-Publication Data

ISBN-10: 979-8-218-35879-2

Printed in USA

To Dee, for all the miles
behind and ahead of us;

to Sally, for your
never-sagging support;

and to That Guy Bob, for being the best
home I can imagine returning to.

Contents

This story's origin story

Sometime in the year before I rode my bike up the East Coast, I emailed my beloved UMass Amherst journalism professor, Norman Sims, to tell him about the trip and that I planned to write about it. He thought I'd be writing some sort of guide to the route. When I told him that I wanted to tell the story of my experience and how the trip felt, he cautioned me, "Well, you have to think about the ending. You can't just hug your friend and walk away." Which is pretty much what happened: Fifty-seven days after leaving Key West, Dee and I hugged on the border of Canada and went back to our lives.

This lack of an ending bothered me. Was there really no story arc, nothing to resolve by the end of my trip? I wasn't a cancer survivor battling my way back to health by pedaling up the coast. I wasn't fighting off crippling depression or running away from abusive family relationships. Dee and I didn't face any huge calamities; we just rode our bikes for two months and I learned to communicate better.

But as time passed, I began to understand that the bike trip had changed me in subtle yet vital ways. Katie Bannon, a wise and gifted editor, read a second draft of my manuscript and pointed out that while the trip itself got a bit redundant—as eight weeks of biking can do—I had learned plenty along the way. Sharing those lessons and how they changed me in short essays made for a better read.

The changes have a lot to do with understanding that life is a journey, not a destination. That's a simple cliché to say but powerful to practice—and hard to truly live for those of us who tend to always look up the road to what's next. More than anything the trip taught me to embrace my sixties and life's third act with all new appreciation and confidence. I've become an evangelist for this phase of life, urging my empty-nester friends to make the most of their time and chase their dreams while they still can.

I wrote about the trip and posted nightly on social media while we were biking. As a result, Dee and I have had the gratifying experience of corresponding with a handful of people, women mostly, who decided that if we—two women approaching sixty and seventy— could pull off this trip, maybe they could too.

Still, this is not a how-to or guidebook for biking the East Coast Greenway. Bicycle touring is my favorite way to experience the world—it's low-budget, eco-friendly travel and low-impact exercise while high on experiences. My dream was to bike way longer than a week's vacation so the traveling would feel more like a way of life. But that was *my* dream; we all harbor aspirations. By sharing insights gained from two months on the road, I hope to nudge you out the door. Walk the Camino, sing or dance or act on stage, build a getaway home—whatever it is, go do that thing you've always wanted to do. It won't be a one-off experience. You will learn about yourself and your capabilities, and this new knowledge will inform the rest of your life.

I'm still a work in progress, but I am savoring the ride.

Our route

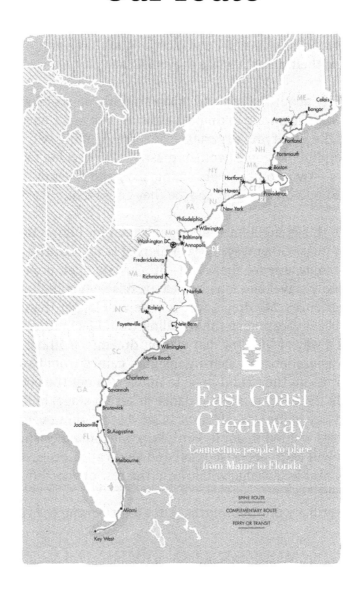

Our itinerary

Key West to the Canadian border on the East Coast Greenway: 2,837 miles, 15 states, 47 days of biking, 8 days off

Day	Destination	Miles
1.	Key West to Marathon, FL	51
2.	Homestead, FL	95
3.	Boca Raton	82
4.	Stuart	82
5.	Melbourne Beach	76
6.	St. Augustine	76
7.	Amelia Island	56
8.	*rest day*	
9.	Brunswick, GA	57
10.	Richmond Hill	66
11.	Savannah	20
12.	Beaufort, SC	59
13.	Charleston	75
14.	Georgetown	76
15.	N. Myrtle Beach	45
16.	Southport, NC	51
17.	*rest day*	
18.	Wilmington to Elizabethtown	62
19.	Fayetteville	61
20.	Clayton	51
21.	Durham	67
22.	*rest day*	
23.	Boydton, VA	69

24.	McKenney	64
25.	Fredericksburg	58
26.	Alexandria	65
27.	*rest day*	
28.	Annapolis, MD	68
29.	Baltimore	34
30.	Havre de Grace	68
31.	Wilmington, DE	46
32.	Philadelphia, PA	43
33.	Princeton, NJ	50
34.	New York City*	38
35.	*rest day*	
36.	*rest day*	
37.	Stamford, CT	47
38.	New Haven	57
39.	West Hartford	57
40.	Putnam	68
41.	Lincoln, RI	57
42.	*rest day*	
43.	South Dartmouth, MA	48
44.	Hyannis	56
45.	Eastham	38
46.	Belmont**	37
47.	*rest day*	
48.	Salem	37
49.	Portsmouth, NH	51
50.	Scarborough, ME	60
51.	Damariscotta	62
52.	Camden	38
53.	Ellsworth	58
54.	Jonesboro	62
55.	Calais	61

* *shortened by commuter train ride*

** *ferry from Provincetown to Boston*

Me and my brother Ron, summer of 1966

INTRODUCTION

Driveway Dreams

The only person you are destined to become
is the person you decide to be.
—Ralph Waldo Emerson

It's early May in the Florida Keys but the afternoon has grown as hot and muggy as an August day in North Carolina. A few road signs confirm what the guy told us at the Cuban sandwich shop a ways back: Seven Mile Bridge looms ahead. My gut starts to clench. Soon we see the long ribbon of two-lane highway, arched in its middle for passing ships, that connects two lumps of land in the Atlantic Ocean. Dee and I are heading north, bicycling on the bridge's shoulder. We guide our tires through road grit and debris, which includes a kitchen knife and, thirty feet later, a cutting board. Cars and trucks thunder past just a few feet to our left. A few feet to our right, a concrete wall not quite as tall as our bike seats is all that stands between us and the ocean. We pedal straight into a stiff, twenty miles-per-hour headwind that slows us to a crawl. I am dehydrated from our forty-five miles of biking already today. From my wrists up to my shoulders, my arms ache from gripping my handlebars too tightly. I'm afraid to change my hand position for fear of swerving into traffic. Have I mentioned that biking over bridges terrifies me?

My odometer says we're down to seven miles an hour. That's easy math: We'll be on this bridge for an hour.

All I can do is pedal. An old children's song comes to mind: *Inch by inch, row by row, gonna make this garden grow.* Those are the only two lines I can call up so I sing them to myself, over and over as I crank my way forward. I'm careful to look just past my front tire. That's my one survival trick for biking across high, scary bridges. With my head down, I try to focus on what's just ahead so I don't consider what's beside and below me, off the edge of the bridge.

Two-thirds of the way across, I grow delirious. I start seeing a chain-link fence rising above the concrete wall and picturing how I could rest by leaning against the fence for a bit. "Dee! I've got to stop," I finally yell over the wind. When she stops and looks back at me, I feel some small relief to see that she, too, looks exhausted. Right up there with my fear of bridges is my worry that I will always be the weakest of my super athletic friends like Dee.

"I've got to wee!" she announces in her distinctive British lilt when I catch up to her. In my traumatized state, I wonder if peeing might help me, too. There's nowhere to hide, just the concrete wall and the car lanes. Dee decides to back up to the wall, crouch down and pee, facing the rushing traffic. I courteously move twenty feet or so downwind from her and crouch down, too. This may be one of the most bizarre scenes I've shared with Dee in our close to four decades of friendship, and normally I'd be doubled over in hysterics. But laughing takes too much energy right now. I pull my shorts back up, slurp some tepid water from a bottle on my bike, take a deep breath, and climb back on my saddle.

This is not at all how things are supposed to be going. It's the first day of our two-month bike ride up the East Coast. The trip is my big hurrah on the brink of turning sixty. For eight weeks I am escaping all the trappings of adult life—job, marriage, parenting, home ownership—to realize a dream I've been fashioning for decades. I want to prove to myself that I am capable of this feat of endurance, biking 3,000 miles from Key West to Canada. But I didn't expect to be tested on day one. I had imagined this first week to be all fun and games, an easy shakedown cruise along the Florida coast full of photo ops and happy texts to our friends and family.

That's how we started the day, laughing over strong Cuban coffee at a Key West cafe and posing for photos at the southernmost buoy. I felt giddy, even cocky about getting underway. We were entertained by iguanas sunning themselves on the bike paths and skittering away just as we approached. We caught vistas of sparkling aquamarine water, an exotic hue that you don't see farther up the East Coast. But the morning sun quickly got oppressive, nothing we were used to yet. Dee lives in Rhode Island and had barely had spring. It had been warmer for me in North Carolina, but nothing like this—the temps were headed for the nineties. Our skin was winter white, our bodies were soft on the saddle. It rained a bit mid-day, making me search for my rain jacket in my panniers. The headwind grew stronger and I got the first flat tire I've had in maybe fifteen years. All on day one! And then this damn bridge.

I don't remember learning how to ride a bike. It seems like I always knew how, but that's not possible; I wasn't a particularly precocious child. My dad probably taught me as a matter of course, when it was my turn and he was ready to set his youngest of five kids off on two wheels. What I do remember is how my bike was my ticket to freedom. Finally, under my own power, I could go places and choose how to get there. Sure, I had to climb some hills. But oh, the flying down! Leaving the confines of our suburban Atlanta neighborhood, I'd cross a busy street and pull up to the public golf course clubhouse, where I bought M&Ms with a dime dropped in a vending machine. Those outings were about as good as it got at age seven or eight.

I was a quirky kid in many ways. I stared out at the world, not saying much but watching intently as my parents and older siblings led their important lives. In my head I was busy creating alternate worlds. Lying on my belly on the family room carpet, I would page through the thick Sears catalog and assemble new families. I'd choose the mom, the dad, and the kids, and then I'd outfit them and their home. I could get lost in this for hours, then thrill to a new season's catalog arriving with all new choices.

On my bike, I'd lose myself to similar dream worlds. While my brother Ron shot baskets on our concrete driveway, I'd circle the perimeter pulling an old wooden wagon behind me. I was leading a covered wagon caravan or driving a train across the country, my stuffed animals as my willing passengers. Later, as an angst-filled adolescent in the suburbs of Baltimore,

I'd hop on my bike and sail off to the Fijis. I'd never actually stepped foot on a sailboat, but I read the book *Dove*, about the handsome sixteen-year-old Robin Graham and how he sailed around the world alone. Sailing joined bicycling as an answer to loneliness, boredom, longing, and uncertainty.

In other ways, I was perhaps not so odd. I was born in 1960, at the tail end of the Baby Boom, into a squarely middle-class family. As a Boomer, I've had plenty of company at every life stage. I graduated from college in the recession of 1982, when we all learned that landing a job just because we had college degrees wasn't a given. I married Bob and we had Kate, our first-born, in 1990, the last peak in U.S. childbirths since the Baby Boom. Now, in my early sixties, I join the throngs of Boomers assessing our prospects, figuring out healthcare, and asking the bigger questions: What has my life meant? How much more can I do? How should I contribute? Is life fun? Am I happy?

For years I had dreamed of an East Coast bike trip as a way to connect the dots of my life, from elementary school in Atlanta to junior high in Baltimore and high school in Boston. I worked a few summers as a camp counselor on Cape Cod and in Maine. I wanted to draw a line from south to north along all those coves and harbors and through favorite cities and know the satisfaction of traveling those miles under my own power. I wanted to take my covered-wagon journey for real.

I define average in so many ways: middle class, late middle age, middle management. Average height,

Day one, leaving Key West. Sally Ann Hay photo

average weight, moderately athletic. All of this pleases the part of me that seeks and values balance. But it also means living a life of mediocrity. The closer I got to sixty, the more restless I felt about the trajectory of my life. I had an itch to do something just a bit extraordinary, one thing that shot up above average. If I didn't push myself to realize a dream now, would I ever?

I had something to prove to the naysayer in my head who has long doubted my ambitions. I didn't need to circle the globe solo to shush my inner critic; biking up the East Coast would do. Most people, dreaming of an epic U.S. bike ride, decide to bike across the country from the Atlantic to the Pacific, or Pacific to the Atlantic. The idea of riding through the desert for days on end and up and over the Rockies sounds kind of how running a marathon sounds these days—not fun, just a test of will and grit. The East Coast would surely offer its share of challenges: headwinds, busy roads with tiny shoulders, bleak stretches of strip malls. But as much as I embrace the beauty of remote settings, I am a child of the suburbs. I find some comfort in never being too far from civilization. I value convenience stores for their bathrooms and coffee machines. I welcome roadside motels for their showers and beds at the end of a long day's ride. I wanted to hug the coast: venturing out on the water without hitting the open sea. I'd prefer to keep the shoreline in sight.

Looking back now, six years since my East Coast trip, I can see how much those two months on my bike taught me. Some things should have been obvious, like the first day's lesson about how adventures don't go exactly to plan, no matter how many months I had spent studying our route, booking accommodations, and collecting gear.

Other lessons run deeper. I am my best self when I travel, or so I always thought. Leaving behind my routine and mundane tasks makes me feel lighter, more optimistic, more aware of my surroundings and entertained by new sights, sounds, and smells. I savor moments more easily than I do at home. Traveling by bike, which I've done in bits and pieces over the years, intensifies this happy traveler effect. I become a kid again, living outdoors all day with no worries except following the route and keeping myself fueled. But living this way for eight weeks, with great expectations riding on the trip, made me face aspects of myself that aren't so appealing, like my irritability, especially when hungry, and my fears, from crossing bridges to doubting myself. To navigate, sometimes literally, so many days and nights with my dear friend, Dee, I had to find my true voice, a delicate balance somewhere between passive and assertive.

Physically I grew stronger with each passing week. That's a beautiful thing about bicycle touring: You train as you go. By the time we reached the halfway point of Washington, DC, I knew I could handle biking sixty miles or so for days on end. It took a little longer—somewhere between New York City and Maine—for things to click in mentally and emotionally. By then, Dee and I were encountering more familiar territory of family and home. After thousands of miles and many weeks of living outdoors in the sun and rain, after crossing plenty of scary bridges and fixing a few flat tires, the wisdom of mindfulness began to take hold. I could see and feel with all my senses how much more the journey matters than getting there. And I started to see how it might be possible to live this way, more confident in my capabilities and open to adventures and possibilities, on and off my bike.

I was talking recently with a friend who is my age, in his early sixties. Michael took a solo motorcycle trip across the country a year before my bike trip. As we compared notes, I used the expression "bucket list." That's not what his trip was about, Michael told me. Rather than checking something off a life list, he rode west on his motorcycle as part of a transition. He was hoping to finally become the person he wants to be, he said. I felt an instant flash of recognition. My bicycle adventure, too, was about becoming who I want to be, finally, as the curtain lifts on life's third act.

Dee (left) and me, feeling punchy before we ran the Boston Marathon as bandits (my first 26.2 miles), April 1986

Find a good friend for the long haul.

You and I have memories
longer than the road
that stretches out ahead
—John Lennon & Paul McCartney,
"The Two of Us"

If you dream of taking adventures but need someone to give you a little push out the door, you need a friend like Dee who just says, "Of course we're going." That's basically what she told me one wintry evening years ago after we cross-country skied along the banks of Boston's Charles River. "We're going to run the Boston Marathon," she announced (back when you could jump in the back of the race without qualifying with a fast enough time at an earlier marathon). She changed my life with that pronouncement, transforming me from a spectator who wondered about doing hard things to an active participant who knew that occasionally she could challenge herself.

I probably wouldn't have biked up the East Coast if Dee wasn't game to go along. Two months is too long to talk to myself while biking all day. At one point I emailed Dee to nail down the trip dates so I could ask my boss about taking a leave of absence. She and I had talked, in theory, about the trip for decades, and we'd been corresponding recently about how this really could be something to plan now that Dee had retired from teaching. But she didn't respond to this particular email for a few weeks, which is not like her.

Did she realize she actually didn't want to spend that much time with me? Could I scramble and piece together chunks of weeks when other friends could ride parts of the route with me? Finally I called Dee. I can't remember if she had missed the email or hadn't seen it as a question that needed to be answered, because she was in. Phew.

But I'm getting ahead of myself. I love the story of how our friendship began. I was twenty-five and pumped up on self importance. I'd just been hired as the assistant editor of Northeastern University's alumni magazine. Since graduating from college with a journalism degree two years earlier, I had held two lowly communications assistant jobs, the last one at a deadly dry municipal planning agency. Now I was returning to the world of journalism, as I envisioned my new job. For the bus ride out to staff orientation at Northeastern's conference center, I picked up a cup of coffee and a *Boston Globe*.

"Ah, that was a good idea," a woman said as I sat down beside her on the bus. She had long blonde hair, a friendly face, and looked to be just a bit older than me. She let me blather on a bit about how my new job would require me to keep up with the news so I was trying to read the newspaper more often.

"I meant the coffee," my seatmate said.

With that, my self-importance burst. We laughed and started chatting. Deirdre Bird was joining Northeastern's business school as a marketing professor. She was new to Boston by way of Purdue, where she earned her doctorate, and South Africa and Rhodesia before that. We learned that we both liked to run and bike, so the following Saturday morning we met up to ride. Leaving our Boston apartments, about a mile from each other, we headed west to Concord for a forty-mile bike ride. I loved it. I had found a playmate.

Over the next few years, Dee and I met on campus a few days a week to take lunchtime runs around the Charles. Weekends typically featured some kind of endurance adventure—a long run, a bike ride, a hike in the mountains. I couldn't always keep up with Dee but she inspired me, and she conveyed confidence in me like all the best teachers do. If I wanted to tag along with her, I had to shrug off most of my self-doubt.

I've described Dee to friends as a cross between Jane Goodall, the English chimpanzee expert, and Joan Benoit Samuelson, the Olympic marathoner. She is tall and lean, with long blond hair when I met her. Back then she dressed for work like the formal British teacher that she was: knee-length skirts, knit tops, and a small neck scarf. The rest of her days she spent in short running shorts, tank tops, and running shoes, always on the move. She has been my navigator, far more adept at reading maps and assessing routes than I am. She has been my chronicler, saving snapshots of our activities in dozens of photo albums neatly labeled and dated.

I met Bob while I was working at Northeastern, too. He was the handsome dark-haired guy in an office down the hall from mine. My crush on him advanced to actual dating. On one lunchtime run with Dee, I told her that Bob was nice and all but I was still considering moving to Singapore. I had this vague idea that I could go halfway around the globe and teach English to inject some adventure into my life. "I don't know, Bob sounds like a good one," Dee said. "You may want to hold onto him."

A year or so later I married him. We had two babies and kept moving farther from Boston and Dee—first to Connecticut, then Ohio, then North Carolina. Meanwhile Dee moved to Rhode Island, started teaching at Providence College, and met Sally. I loved Sally as soon as I met her. She's wise and kind, not much into athletics, and she seemed to offer Dee some grounding. With Sally, my globetrotting friend was ready to settle down. They married and have lived in Rhode Island ever since.

We stayed in touch with letters and emails, occasionally meeting for week-long bike trips and road races. In Ohio I found running pals who pushed me to run the Cleveland marathon to try to qualify for Boston officially. Dee and Sally came to Ohio so Dee could run Cleveland with us. We all qualified and ran Boston the next year, a few days before my fortieth birthday. That marathon was the peak of my physical achievements. I still run, but I've gotten slower every year since. At fifty I gave up marathons. That one moment of athletic legitimacy at forty still makes me proud. I'm glad I got to share it with the friend who first talked me into running 26.2 miles.

My dreams of a bike ride up the East Coast always included riding with Dee. Our biking pace was compatible from the start. We bring similar tourist mind-sets, more interested in what we see than how fast we go. In many ways, the bike trip was a tame adventure for Dee. She has biked the length of the West Coast, a much more challenging route, solo. She has hitch-hiked across South America and bushwhacked through Africa. She has sailed around the world three times as a faculty member on Semester at Sea. She's run too many Boston Marathons for me to count. Bike for two months, staying in motels and friends' houses? No problem.

Road signs started popping up saying it was time to plan this trip for real. In December 2016, Dee retired from teaching, freeing her schedule. A month earlier I joined the staff of the East Coast Greenway Alliance, the nonprofit organization working to develop the route that we planned to follow. My work was to share the organization's news and to tell stories of the people who use the Greenway and who champion its growth. My first-hand experiences on the route would certainly enhance my work—as I told Dennis, my boss, in pitching my two-month leave.

I felt a bit of urgency as I watched us age. At sixty-seven and fifty-eight, Dee and I weren't as spry as we once were. Dee had grown far thinner, making her look deceptively weak. While she was losing weight I was finding it, unfortunately, swaddling my body in classic middle-age extra pounds. Dee was fighting a bad Achilles tendon; my right knee was cranky. We'd have to make room in our bike bags for eyeglasses and contact solution, sunscreen and anti-inflammatories. But cycling doesn't pound your joints, and we would pace ourselves. We were marathoners (well, former ones), in it for the long haul.

We spent a winter comparing notes by email. We both bought sturdy new touring bikes and waterproof panniers, the double saddlebags you carry behind you on a bike rack, for our clothes and gear. I created a spreadsheet and broke up the route into roughly sixty-mile days, then split the work between us of reaching out to friends and relatives who might put us up for a night as we pass through. Otherwise we booked nights at roadside motels and Airbnbs. Nothing says adventure like hitting the open road with a Google Sheet on your iPad that tells you where you'll stay each night, right? But I was hoping to email and text as little as I could while we biked; it's one of the trappings of civilization that I was fleeing.

I worried about a few things in the countdown to our trip including what two months together, just the two of us, would feel like. We'd never spent that much time living together day after day. The longest bike trip I had taken then was a week, and always in the company of others, not just Dee.

Most importantly, we weren't the same people we were back in our twenties and thirties, when the adventurous Dee was my teacher and I was the eager learner. I had grown up some, with more confidence thanks to years of being a wife and mom. We'd both grown more set in our ways. What happens, I wondered, if we get tired of each other after a few weeks?

In Savannah, ten days into the trip, we had dinner with my coworker Brent, who was coordinating the South Carolina and Georgia stretches of the East Coast Greenway. Waiting for us to get to the restaurant, he told some women who work with his wife about us and our trip. "Oh!" the women called out when Dee and I showed up, "You're the badass women!"

Brent suggested we should get that tattoo when we finished the ride. He got us.

Despite all the laughs and fun days, a bit of tension began to brew early in the trip, I'm embarrassed to admit. While the biking each day was magically different, a sense of mundane routine about our mornings and evenings set in. Unpacking and repacking our panniers, washing our clothes as we showered and air drying them overnight, scrounging for breakfast and dinner—these daily chores began to weigh on me. I'm not a fan of repetition and routine in general. When I'm cranky—mostly tired, hungry, or both—I can fixate on weird things, little things that inexplicably become big deals. Mind you, I didn't consider what odd habits of mine might be bugging Dee. But as I grew prickly in the evenings and mornings, parts of her daily routines began to annoy me.

Coffee, for instance. I quickly ceded morning coffee responsibilities to Dee. She prefers her coffee piping hot, with cream (not white powder!), and she needs it to be decaf, which isn't always easy to find. We'd be checking into a motel and she'd already be scanning the lobby for their coffee station and for creamers she could collect for our stash. She'd ask motel maids for a few extra Keurig cups from their carts while we were pushing our bikes into our room. Camel that she is, she would down three or four cups each morning while I finished two. Dee may have felt she was being gracious by making coffee for me each morning, but I felt oddly controlled. I was accustomed to making my own coffee every other morning of my life.

At the end of our third week we arrived at my house in Durham for two nights and a day off. After waking up in my own bed, I was ridiculously excited to make coffee in my own French press in my own kitchen. I worked quietly, with Dee still downstairs in our guest room. I poured the rest of last night's decaf from the French press into a mug for her, knowing she'd be happy to microwave it for her first cup of the day. I put the teapot on to boil and measured out three scoops of my favorite coffee, Starbucks dark roast Verona, into the French press. Then, waiting for the water to boil, I went outside to retrieve the morning paper.

In just that time, Dee had come upstairs and was standing at the kitchen sink. She turned to look at me as I walked back to the kitchen. She covered her mouth, apologetic. "Lisa, I've done a horrible thing!" she said. She had emptied out the fresh scoops of coffee, thinking it was last night's.

I erupted. "Dee! This is my house! I just wanted to make coffee in my house!" I pretended to be kidding, but I wasn't entirely. While I could almost laugh about feeling so irritated about such a little thing, part of me wanted to shove Dee out of my kitchen. So much for being selfless, easygoing, and low maintenance, mi casa es su casa and all, the way I want to see myself. Or maybe we all have our breaking points. It turns out mine, or one of mine, is owning my French press in my house after being away for three weeks.

Our biggest stressor during the day was finding our way. On our phones, we could follow either the East Coast Greenway route on one app—a red line running the 3,000 miles along the coast —or Google Maps for bikes, which sometimes followed the greenway route and sometimes suggested shorter options. Google Maps offers more context, showing amenities like grocery stores or coffee shops we may be passing. I wanted to see as much of the greenway as I could, being loyal to my employer. I also wanted to navigate sometimes—to lead, literally—just to know that I could. But Dee is much better at it. She has a natural sense of direction and better vision. While I needed to stop and find my glasses to study the map, Dee toggled easily between the two phone apps with one hand while biking—an admirable feat of coordination and balance.

Halfway through our trip, we had a longish ride leaving Washington, D.C., and heading to Annapolis. It was a fun ride out of the city on the Anacostia Trail before the roads became rural and rolling. The air was humid with clouds gathering. As the skies got darker and we encountered "road closed" and detour signs, we started studying our maps.

I'm not very proud of the next few hours as my mood kept deteriorating. It was a sad cocktail of threatening skies, tough hills, and navigation stress. I led for most of the afternoon but finally agreed that Dee's Google Maps option looked better for getting us to our destination sooner, with looming clouds and all the detour signs. Dee pulled in front and I rode behind her, a bit petulant. I worried the route would take us on a busy, scary road. That's part of my issue with Google Maps for bikes: I don't always trust its choices. I was tired of taking shortcuts off the greenway route, but I was also nervous about getting drenched in a thunderstorm.

Dee was either oblivious to or ignoring my churlish mood, or both, as she rode ahead. We were five miles or so from our destination when she spotted signs for a Greek festival. passed a long line of cars parked along the side of the road. It was one of those sprawling mega church-school complexes that often sprout in suburbia. Dee suggested we stop and get something to eat because we didn't know if there would be any food to find where we were staying.

"That's fine," I told her, sullen. "I'm not really hungry [which is hardly ever true], but I'll go sit somewhere."

I had no interest in the scene: Hundreds of suburbanites milling around under tents as we wandered in, sweaty and gritty and not from around there. I felt like a party crasher at some big family wedding or some high school's end-of-year party. I didn't want to stand in long lines. I didn't want to eat Greek food. I was tired of listening to Dee enthusiastically tell strangers all about our trip—maybe because I felt I could tell it better? Deep down, I'm afraid, I just wanted to control the narrative.

I found an empty table and sat down with my water bottle. Mostly, I needed to get over myself. I had been craving some time alone, which had been in short supply the last four weeks. And I got it, ten minutes or so of quiet mindlessness before Dee showed up. She was happy to have scored some baklava at a bargain price. She split it in half to share with me. I was relieved that it wasn't grape leaves or some other Greek dish that I don't really like, even on a good day when I'm not being childish.

Sugar always helps. That night we were pleasantly surprised to be wined and well dined, appetizers through dinner and dessert, by our incredibly generous overnight host. The conversation gained steam when we learned Cindy shared our political views. I started to grasp how the company of hosts and friends eased the intensity of it just being Dee and me, day and night. Consider this, as we told people: After sleeping in the same room—sometimes the same bed, if we had to—night after night, we rode all day within a few feet of each other. This is more togetherness than Bob and I experience in a week. Having other people to tell our stories to and offering new conversational threads helped. Back on the road the next day, we could chew on their stories and ideas.

One night further north, in a hotel room in Delaware, I summoned up my courage and did a brave thing. Once again I had been growing irritated by little things. But instead of becoming quiet or passive aggressive—the paths I usually choose—I was determined to make a healthier choice. I asked Dee if we could talk before we headed out to dinner.

"You are so smart," I told her. "Your brain and your body move so quickly. I don't move that quickly, and I don't always want to." I told her about how often she instructed me on how to open a door with my bike, where to put my coffee cup or how to throw it away, all because she was three steps ahead of me. "It makes me feel like you think I'm a bumbling idiot because you have to show me how to do things, but really I just don't do things as quickly as you do."

"I don't think you're an idiot!" Dee responded, genuinely surprised. She noted that I had competently planned this trip.

I explained that's how it feels when someone repeatedly instructed me this way. I was drawing on what I could remember about healthy conflict resolution from when our kids were teenagers. It's effective to use "I" words and share how you feel, as I recalled.

This was scary new territory for me. Typically if I was starting to feel tension like this with a friend, I would just start to withdraw, choosing to see them less rather than be brave enough to speak up. But in the middle of this bike trip I didn't have the option of withdrawing. And Dee isn't any friend. She and I have a rich shared history of decades of adventures and the promise of more adventures ahead as our time frees up in retirement. Navigating my emotions with her was as critical as getting the route right on the road. Screwing up would feel disastrous.

Dee responded so reasonably that she left me in awe. She said she understood what I was saying and she appreciated me speaking up. She said these things genuinely, without the sarcasm or edge that would be common in my family. I thought immediately of my sisters and how they would be proud of me for having this conversation. None of us learned much about conflict communications when we were growing up. When our mother got unhappy, she'd turn her laser focus outward, making it clear that someone else—our dad or one of us kids—was the source of her misery. She would slam cabinets and doors and barely speak, then finally let loose on whoever she was furious with. For years Bob has helped me learn to address issues when they happen instead of letting them fester and boil over that way. It seems appropriate for spouses to work on their communication issues. But friends? Aren't we just supposed to enjoy each other's company?

Speaking my mind, and having Dee respond without friction, instantly cleared the air. We headed out to a brand new downtown Wilmington restaurant that we spotted coming into town. We walked into great excitement: An eating contest pitted the restaurant owners against local radio personalities. It was a loud party with lots of cheering and jeering. One of the owners visited our table and told us that his place had only been open eleven weeks but had already made a splash. He didn't win the spicy wings contest; a burly radio guy finished his plateful first. Our new friend looked a little rough from the challenge so we urged him to go home. Saying goodbye to each of us separately, he took our hands in his and wished us—as so many new friends had over those weeks—safe travels. It felt like a fine resolution to the day's turbulence.

I started the last day of our East Coast ride with a familiar sense of anxiety, the kind of dread I used to feel on the morning of a marathon. Why, after riding all this way, did a fifty-five-mile day suddenly feel daunting? Nerves, Dee said. She felt something similar. She had a terrible night's sleep, like it was the night before a marathon.

Yesterday's downpours had stopped. The sky was overcast but calm. Marla, the manager of the Blueberry Patch, gave us blueberry muffins, yogurt, and coffee in the motel lobby along with a little road intelligence. Cooper Mountain will be a doozy of a downhill, she told us. So that gave me something to stew about for our first twenty miles or so. What if I fly down a steep mountain and flip over my bike on our last day? Kindly, happily, our route turned right when the road to Cooper Mountain went straight.

We had a picnic at about thirty miles on the steps of the Dennysville town office, which is a trailer with a handicapped-access ramp, because there was nothing else around for miles. It was one of our quietest and most remote rides of the trip. We mostly had the road to ourselves. Rolling hills, thick woods, pretty streams. The last ten or so miles before Calais were even more remote as we entered the Moosehorn National Wildlife Refuge. We got weird texts on our phones welcoming us to Canada. Dee noticed that her phone had jumped an hour ahead to Canadian time. We waved away a few black flies and rolled over a few more hills before hitting Route 1.

Soon I spotted a traffic circle up ahead, signaling that we were on the outskirts of town. As we got closer we could read a big sign planted in the middle of the traffic circle, "Welcome to Calais." Whoa! The sign hit me harder than I expected it to: We'd done it! Two months, 2,900 miles, done. It was real, not a dream. We pulled our bikes over to the circle's curb and posed them together, the Calais sign behind them, both of us working our cameras. I turned and gave Dee a hug. I realized that, oddly enough, this was our first hug of the trip. Was it really the first time I felt we had something to celebrate? Had I been holding my breath for two months to see if we'd make it? My tears started, a sure sign that my emotions were bigger than any words or thoughts could express.

We still had an official photo op a mile or two ahead of us where Sally was waiting in a parking lot on the banks of the St. Croix River, which separates Maine

Photo finish: Trying unsuccessfully to lift our heavy bikes overhead in Calais, Maine, along the St. Croix River. Sally Ann Hay photo

from Canada. Then Sally would drive us home to Rhode Island, and I would take Amtrak home to North Carolina and Bob.

If we are lucky, Dee and I have years adventures ahead of us—runs and rides, trips and visits. Sniffling quietly as we biked into Calais, I took it all in and felt sheer, uncomplicated pride at how far my friend and I have traveled, in every sense of the word.

A few years ago on the North Carolina coast, close to our thirty-third anniversary. Kate Malekoff photo

LESSON 2

Find a spouse who knows you need to leave home sometimes.

All of these lines across my face
Tell you the story of who I am
So many stories of where I've been
And how I got to where I am
But these stories don't mean anything
When you've got no one tell them to
It's true: I was made for you.
— Brandi Carlile, "The Story"

I met Bob the same year I met Dee, when all three of us were working at Northeastern University. At twenty-five I thought I was getting old. I was editing a magazine, my dream since college, even if it was an alumni magazine. I had broken things off with my college boyfriend because I felt more like his caretaker than girlfriend. There I was, an untethered career woman in Boston, ready to date men—only I never really learned how to date. Plus, I wasn't finding many men in my age group. At Northeastern, it seemed as though most of the men were either undergraduates or middle-aged professors.

I had barely spoken with him but I had a huge crush on That Guy Bob, as all my coworkers knew. He was the handsome guy, appropriately aged somewhere between twenty-five and forty, who worked down the long hall of our office suites. Word was that a few women in the building also had set their sights on him. I'd have put my bets on the Jamie Lee Curtis look-alike at the end of the hall because she was tall like Bob and stylish. Still, my crush persisted. I'd report back to my coworkers every time we passed in the hall and said hi to each other.

At some point I sent our photographer's administrative assistant down the hall to gather intelligence. She reported back that he was working at the center while going to grad school at Harvard (smart!). He used to coach soccer and lacrosse at Princeton (I love soccer and lacrosse, I played in high school; not very well but still!). He was thirty-one (older, but not too old). And as far as anyone knew, he was single.

One morning Bob and I happened to walk up the stairs to our offices at the same time. I was embarrassed because my hair was wet. But I forced myself to carry on our first conversation, short but chatty. As he stopped to head left to his office, he held out his hand.

"I'm Bob, by the way," he said.

"Bob?" I repeated, suppressing a giggle. *I know your whole resumé.* "Hi, I'm Lisa."

We started to date in September. I ran my second marathon that fall, partly thinking it would impress him. But it turns out I've never had to play games like that with Bob. I've been able to just be myself.

The dream of biking up the East Coast took root sometime in my twenties and hung out for years in the back of my mind's overstuffed closet, like a forgotten favorite sweater waiting for the right occasion. I was busy raising kids, moving homes, and meeting work deadlines. Even as an empty nester, the idea of taking two months off and leaving Bob and our two dogs to go ride my bike seemed a bit selfish. But the older I get, the more selfishness is morphing into self-care. If there's ever a time to figure out what I want, it's now.

"You should do it," Bob would say whenever we talked about it in the few years before I left. He has an impressive track record of supporting me that way, understanding my need to reach certain goals even if it makes things harder for him. Training for a handful of marathons in my forties meant I was often fatigued and gone from home more, leaving Bob with the kids for my long training runs and race weekends away with pals. He seemed to understand that it balanced the parenting scales a bit, because his job as a college athletic director meant he had to be away plenty of nights and weekends for games and meetings.

But with our kids grown and living in New York City, they don't need much from me now more than texting them the occasional affirmation in response to a bad day and paying their cell phone bill. And Bob? He knows how much I love to bike and how badly I wanted to ride all of the East Coast. Ours has never been a relationship where we tell the other person what they can or can't do. And after living together for more than thirty years, we should be able to survive eight weeks apart.

At the end of our second day of riding, Dee and I arrived at a weird Airbnb in Homestead, Florida. Inside a generic home in a newer, generic development, an elderly Chinese couple greeted us, speaking no English. Upstairs our key opened one of a number of closed bedroom doors. We found a spacious, generic suite with two queen beds and a huge bathroom with whirlpool bath and shower.

"Would you mind terribly if I scoot into the shower first?" Dee asked.

Sure, I told her. Because all I wanted was to collapse on the carpeted floor and moan. We had biked for 10 hours and nearly 100 miles in heat and headwinds. Sometimes it felt like we would never leave the wilds of the Florida Keys. Despite lavish amounts of sunscreen, I was sunburned. Worse yet, I saw the beginnings of a heat rash, my body's distress signal. I hadn't biked this far in maybe a year, and not in such heat.

I called Bob in this state of despair. "Uh, I don't know what to say," he said, helpless. "I don't think I've ever heard you sound so bad."

I don't know why I called him. Did I really need Bob to know how hard the day was? He and I don't communicate very well on the phone as it is, when one of us is away. He often sounds distracted, like he's multitasking. He repeats things he has told me the day before, like when his plane is due back in town. He's not all that interested in the smaller details of my day; he's just listening to hear whether things are OK or not.

Lesson learned that day: It's not fair to call home when you're really down and out and there's nothing Bob can do about it. Better to send light, funny texts and photos from the road, as I did most days going forward.

A week or so later, I was sitting on the porch of a coffee shop in downtown Beaufort, South Carolina. We ended our day's ride on the beautiful Spanish Moss Trail, which brought us just a block from our Airbnb. I was in a far more cheerful mood when I caught Bob on the phone.

"It's been beautiful," I told him of the last few days of riding. "I really need to work on savoring all these moments because they are flying by so quickly."

Bob laughed. "I wouldn't say the days are exactly flying by," he told me. He was counting days the other way, wishing they would speed up and I'd come home.

I was sorry that Bob's days were too quiet now that his teaching had wrapped up for the semester. Work has been central to his life. He doesn't have hobbies, really, and he's grown less likely in recent years to reach out to initiate seeing friends. But I also savored the fact that Bob had, in his backhanded way, just told me he loves me.

Three weeks into the ride, we reached my home in Durham for two nights and a day. In the comfort of all things familiar, including Bob, I felt energized. In the morning, while Dee saw a friend from one of her Semester at Sea voyages, Bob and I went to Ninth Street Bakery, one of my favorite Durham places, for breakfast. I felt a tiny distance from him. I guessed it was because he knew the visit was quick and temporary; Dee and I had another five weeks of pedaling north.

The next morning, packing up to leave, my heart was split down the middle. I was sad to be leaving Bob and all things comfortable, but I was also excited to get back on the road. That's a good place to be, I decided. I'd only worry if the balance were tilted to either side, if I didn't want to ride again or if I was in a hurry to leave home.

Bob had admitted that the house had been quieter than ever these last few weeks. That was his chief complaint with my trip: He didn't have much going on. Meanwhile Sally was experiencing a social whirlwind in Rhode Island with lots of her friends and Dee's friends checking on her and inviting her to lunches and dinners. I wished Bob had some of that.

At the end of our day in Havre de Grace, Maryland, Dee and I walked across the highway from our motel to CVS so Dee could make a photo card for Sally from one of her hundreds of trip photos so far. She had been sending off cards to Sally regularly along with nearly daily phone calls, which is far more communications than Bob and I had shared. Inspired by her photo card, I decided to buy an anniversary card for Bob and send it, a week or so ahead of our actual date. He would be shocked to get my mail. Along with talking on the phone, we aren't very good about things like celebrating our anniversary, especially when one of us is traveling.

Our decades together feel much like our wedding did: nontraditional. June 13, 1987, was the hottest, steamiest day in Boston that whole year I think, after a cold and dreary spring. We said our vows in a clearing in the woods in the presence of family, friends, and a rumpled justice of the peace who arrived late. We retreated quickly to a conference center lodge for a laid-back celebration. A few guys got a game of horseshoes going out on the lawn; three little boys had their dress shirts off within the first hour. And so our lives have proceeded. Through two kids, five dogs, moves to four states and let's not count the houses and jobs, these constants remain in our lives: Don't do anything stuffy, have few rules or have-tos, and treasure your friends. We've done the hard work of learning how to argue with each other, how to listen, how to keep an open mind, even how to take care to wipe the counters or close the bag of crackers just because it matters to the other person. Bob would say one of us still has some room for improvement in those last areas.

The nicest thing my mother—never one to be warm and fuzzy about relationships—ever said about our marriage was that Bob and I certainly gave each other space. I'm sure she was looking at us from the perspective of someone who married in 1950, when household gender roles were so much more defined. While the demands of Bob's work in college athletics meant that I did the bulk of raising our kids while always working at least part-time, he gave me the time and space for my friends and our pursuits. Our marriage feels like an equal partnership with plenty of mutual respect—which perhaps we should acknowledge more than we do.

Years ago, when we were living in Mystic, Connecticut, and the kids were young, Dee came to visit. The lightbulb had just clicked on that she liked women and she brought her first girlfriend with her for the weekend. That relationship didn't last long, I'm happy to say; the woman was a bit of a know-it-all. Watching Bob pack for a work trip, the girlfriend told me that it looked like it was hard for Bob to leave home and I should tuck love notes into his suitcase when he has to go away. Bob and I have laughed about that idea ever since. If one of us ever receives a surprise love note or flowers from the other, we'll immediately grow suspicious.

As we neared the end of our trip in north coastal Maine, our wifi reception got spotty. We had a few more days to ride and I had a sense that we'd keep getting further off the grid. I texted my family to say I might be out of touch but I was due to finish the ride in two days and that I loved them. Later that morning their responses brought instant tears. Kate wished me good luck. Tommy said he was proud and jealous. Bob told me I was a badass.

I cry easily when emotions overwhelm me. Not loud, dramatic sobs, just quiet crying. At our finish line photo op in Calais, Maine, I kept wiping away little tears and sniffling quietly. Sally, always the caretaker, was puzzled; her partner, Dee, is not one to cry in moments like this. "Do you have allergies?" Sally asked. I didn't have words right at the moment so I couldn't explain myself very well. I was simply overwhelmed, feeling it all at the end of our adventure.

I was surprised by how much I wished Bob was there. I wouldn't have had to say much. He would just see my tears and get it. He would hug me hard and tell me he was proud. And he would find some way to make me laugh.

A long time before that it seems (but it had only been two months), Bob drove with me to our little house on the Neuse River to drop off the dogs. Marylou and Nancy, dear friends from Ohio, arrived as the first shift of week-long dog sitters. Miraculously, I had enlisted eight weeks' worth of friends to watch Amos and Juno at the river so Bob wouldn't have to manage the dogs himself for two months. We had a fun evening with our friends, then Bob and I had to head back to Durham the next day. Bob had been talking a big game about how he needed me to drive the three hours home because he had so many papers to grade. But when it came time to actually leave my friends and say goodbye to the dogs, a tsunami of emotion and tears overwhelmed me. The pain of leaving my pups surprised me. Bob took one look at me and said, "I'll drive." It was all I needed.

At the end of my trip, after a marathon eighteen-hour train ride from Rhode Island, Bob and I had a fun reunion in Durham. We didn't have much to say, we just felt happy and relieved. Part of me wouldn't relax, though, until I saw the dogs again. They were still at the river house, this week in the care of my sister-in-law, Adrienne. We headed there first thing the next morning. Amos and Juno greeted me with lots of hard tail wagging and circling around my legs. I could tell they had done fine during their two-month river camp, well attended to by each week's new set of caregivers. I was grateful for all those who helped, and I was so happy to see those babies.

Back at our house in Durham, the dogs acted as if they never left. Amos took up his post at our front fence again, sounding the alert when anyone walked by. Juno spent the day curled up in her favorite chair. Amos walked back and forth along the side of our bed, using the bedspread to scratch his sides. Juno scavenged for trash on our walks with renewed gusto.

It shouldn't surprise me how easily the dogs returned to their patterns. They are creatures of habit, they love routine. I have my own habits: I was back to playing Pandora mornings and nights on my phone or laptop; I had missed my music. I was running the same routes I used to run, although running felt a little strange after two months off. And I was climbing into bed at night as soon after 8 p.m. as I could. Loving going to bed never changes.

People kept asking what my next adventure would be. I knew they expected me to tell them about another long-distance trip with Dee: West Coast? Canada? I told them what I felt strongly: My next longish trip would be with Bob, biking or not. He was patient and supportive while I was gone for two months. On the delicate balance scales of life that I care so much about, the bike trip tilted toward self-care. I earned that time away to chase my dream after decades of parenting and work. But to leave Bob again for more such adventures, at least in the near future, would tip the scales more toward selfishness.

For those first few days back together, we enjoyed vacation time at the river and treated each other kindly, on good behavior. But soon enough Bob pointed out that a glass didn't get very clean in the dishwasher and told me how I could have prevented that.

"I guess the honeymoon's over," he laughed.

Making me laugh is one of the best things That Guy Bob does. He also never lets me take myself too seriously, which is important for someone who tends to get boggled up in her mind, strategizing and analyzing things to death. Yet he understands when I need to push myself, and he welcomes me back home from adventures. For better or worse, richer or poorer, in sickness and health, Bob loves me, laughs with me, and does my sweaty laundry.

Rover, fully loaded, enjoying a rest stop by the water

LESSON 3

Buy a sturdy bike and pack lightly.

On the road again
Goin' places that I've never been
Seein' things that I may never see again
And I can't wait to get on the road again
—Willie Nelson, "On the Road Again"

Having a good bike that fit me well and just enough gear, not too much, were nearly as important as having a good friend to share the ride with. One of the many things I've always loved about riding my bike, and especially traveling by bike, is the simplicity. It's just me, my bike, and whatever I've packed into my handlebar bag and panniers and we're off to see the world. A bike loaded with bags weighs more, certainly, but speed isn't the point when you're touring. Meanwhile, all you need is right at hand. If it starts to rain, you can grab your rain jacket. Need a Bandaid? There are some in your toiletries bag in your left pannier.

You learn to pare down your definition of necessities, knowing that the less you carry the less you have to pull. I saw a funny social media meme recently that showed a touring bike with bags parked in front of a big ol' RV. The caption read something like, *We have different definitions of 'all we need.'*

I bought my first-ever touring bike a few months ahead of our East Coast trip. I knew my beat-up road bike, with its skinny tires and lighter frame, wouldn't be up to the challenge. Shopping for my new ride shook up everything I'd known about biking. Instead of focusing on lighter and faster, I had to think about comfort and sturdiness. I chose a Kona Rove, a heavy aluminum bike built to handle the miles and various surfaces while carrying my bags. The first thing I loved about it was its wider tires, about twice the width of a road bike. I could ride easily over grassy strips and gravel paths where skinny tires would be skittish. The wider tires also luxuriously cushion the ride. No more clipping into pedals with biking shoes, either—with all the stops and starts of riding though towns, the bit of speed you gain from clipping in is negligible. I could wear far more comfortable sneakers, even sturdy sandals. And just like that, my days of caring how fast I ride were over. I won't ever go back to riding a road bike.

You could see touring bikes as a bit like sensible shoes. I love how my everyday Merrell clogs offer comfort and support, and I think they look hippie-chic in their own way. My daughter, Kate, rolls her eyes every time I buy a new pair. She's in her thirties, which is a fine time for wearing flats with pointed toes. I won't ever go back there, either. And to me, my bike is handsome. The brownish coppery paint has faint sparkles in it. The bike shop added retro-style fenders to keep rain spit and mud splatter off my back side. Online I found multi-colored handlebar tape in a woven, faintly ethnic pattern, a bit of colorful bling that made Rover even more distinctive. After a dozen or so years of riding a black, scratched-up Raleigh road bike, it was fun to ride a shiny new bike that people stopped to ooh and ahh over.

When you meet up to ride, cyclists are notorious for checking out your bike top to bottom before they look at you. I have no idea what those quick assessments take in. I'm not a gear head; frames and components mean little to me. I can tell you what color the bike is. It reminds me of a favorite scene in Bill Bryson's book, *A Walk in the Woods,* about hiking the Appalachian Trail. Bryson is decidedly not a gear guy. He dreads the inevitable attempt at gear talk when guys would approach him in the trail shelters. "Say, why did you pick that backpack?" they'd ask, looking to launch a conversation about equipment and brands. Bryson would cut them off with, "I suppose so I wouldn't have to carry all my stuff in my arms."

Of all the bike gear I brought on the East Coast trip, which wasn't much, my odometer was my most valued accessory. Mounting a device on your bike to measure distance and speed is old school, because most cyclists use a phone app for that. But I've had an odometer on each of my bikes since I was a kid, and I take the same pleasure in watching my miles grow now as I did when I was twelve. Phone apps can give you lots of data: your average and top speed, your heart rate, calories burned, probably what you had for breakfast. I knew I'd be using my phone for navigation on the trip but I didn't completely trust the technology—what if I lost battery power? Or have to turn my phone off in the rain? My odometer collects loads of data, including my CO_2 offset and other metrics I don't understand. I kept my little device, the size of a book of matches, on one screen that showed my accumulated mileage (so I had to do math every day) and a smaller indicator of current speed.

Dee in her high-tech raingear—a plastic poncho—as she sorts out the route in Maine on our second to last day.

Shortly before we left for Florida, I gave my bike its name, Rover. It's an extension of its make, Rove. Plus its coppery brown color reminded me of Amos, my sweet bigger dog. I feel some of the same unconditional love for my bike that I do for my dogs. Bikes and dogs: They're reliable, handsome, there for you. Dee does not share my proclivity for anthropomorphizing. Her poor bike barely had a name. It, too, is a Kona

Rove, but it's the high-end steel version in a tasteful indigo blue. She half-heartedly calls it Steel. Rover is male; Steel has an indistinct gender identity. They/them.

We both packed as lightly as we could. Our handlebar bags carried our wallets, snacks, sunscreen, and other important stuff. In two rear panniers, I carried two sets of clothes for riding. I had a few warm layers for evening chill. a few things to wear after riding, and my beloved pajama pants; an iPad for writing nightly blog posts; a small set of toiletries; one extra tire tube and a few bike tools; and one big tube of sunscreen. I didn't carry much else other than food and two water bottles. But still Dee and I found things to leave behind at three weeks when we reached my house in Durham: a book, an extra shirt, a sweatshirt. Once we started climbing hills, everything got re-evaluated for whether it was truly worth its weight.

For this trip, I officially gave up bike shorts with their chamois padding. The feeling of walking around wearing a diaper is supposed to be the trade-off for protecting your tender areas. Mine get irritated either way. So instead I bought two comfortable pairs of shorts made with a soft, quick drying fabric with long legs and two pockets. I just had to get through a few stages of adjustment. In the first few days it's a searing pain with what feels like blistery wounds on tender inner skin. It stings in the shower and every time I pee. But within a few days the skin heals and the pain starts to fade. Too much information, you may be thinking? There's no such thing on a bike trip. We are in this together.

Dee waits on a shadeless stretch of the East Coast Greenway in Florida while I snap a picture of my favorite logo.

LESSON 4

You don't have to blaze your own trail.

Every day is a winding road
I get a little bit closer
Every day is a faded sign
I get a little bit closer to feeling fine
—Sheryl Crow, "Every Day Is a Winding Road"

While I had dreamed about biking up the East Coast for decades, I only learned about the East Coast Greenway in my fifties. It was an exciting finding: A group of forward-thinking planners and transportation advocates from Boston and New York met in the early 1990s to map out a route from Boston to Washington, DC, beginning with existing bike paths and finding low-traffic roads to connect them. The greenway—a more inclusive term than bike path, meaning it's for walkers, runners, cyclists, rollerskaters, and all—kept growing, stretching now from the Canadian border in Maine to the southernmost tip in Key West, Florida.

Close to forty percent of those 3,000 miles are now on safe, protected paths away from motorized traffic. The rest is still in development. It's slow and expensive work that involves convincing each municipality along the route to find the funding—an average of $1 million per mile—to complete its stretch.

I love many things about the East Coast Greenway, including that the route intentionally takes you through cities big and small: Miami, Savannah, Charleston, Raleigh, Richmond, Washington DC, Baltimore, Philadelphia, New York, Hartford, Providence, Boston, Portland. Other bike touring routes loop you far from urban areas, thinking you don't want to mess with the traffic and such. But riding into these cities was one of my favorite parts of our trip. Who knew there were beautifully designed greenways carrying you delightfully, and safely, into and out of Miami, Manhattan, Philadelphia, and more? When you only drive into those cities, you assume Interstate 95 is the only way to get there. The East Coast Greenway's founders wanted the route to serve local pedestrians and bike commuters heading to work in big cities as well as touring cyclists.

Learning that the East Coast Greenway Alliance, the nonprofit working to develop the route, was based in Durham, North Carolina, where Bob and I moved in 2005, seemed incredibly providential. I was working as communications director at a public boarding high school in Durham, a job and community I loved, when a similar position opened with the alliance. They needed all the work I'd been doing for nonprofits: updating the website, writing blog posts, sending a monthly newsletter, and posting on social media. The opportunity to do that work for a cause so near and dear to my heart was almost too good to be true.

A few years into the job, after launching a new website and helping with two months of twenty-fifth anniversary celebrations, I asked my boss if I could take two months to bike the route. I knew my experience would infuse my work with more energy—not to mention taking some valuable snapshots from the route. But mostly I wanted to realize my dream.

On our trip, Dee would laugh at how quickly I could spot the green and blue ECG signs telling us where to turn. Seeing the greenway logo was like spotting your state's license plate on a car halfway across the country—a touch of home! It also usually meant we'd be turning off a noisy road onto a pretty bike path where we didn't have to worry about car traffic and we could hear each other talk. Blissful.

I used to look at greenways and bike paths with disdain. Those are for people walking with baby strollers, I'd think, not for serious cyclists. That was in my short-lived era of thinking my miles per hour were the most important thing about a bike ride. They aren't. And it was also in the days before cell phones and distracted driving. Now I champion safe, multi-use greenways, especially the well-designed ones.

These days, my greenway passion shapes my travels, even where I live. Last year Bob and I bought a little house in Barrington, Rhode Island, so we could spend our summers in New England. The house is nothing special but it sits two houses away from a beautiful pond and the East Bay Bike Path, a piece of the complementary East Coast Greenway route out to Cape Cod. I've biked and run on the East Bay Bike Path for years. It's perhaps the prettiest bike path I've seen.

Our friends never get why we're so excited about our new place until they join us on some part of the fourteen miles running along the Narragansett Bay from Providence to Bristol. The former rail line follows the bay while passing scenic coves, crossing a few rivers, and offering trailside and nearby coffee and ice cream shops in little town centers.

If you want to travel even more miles of planned bike routes, Europe is miles, or kilometers, ahead of the United States. Visit Amsterdam and Copenhagen, London and Paris, to understand the possibilities of putting bikes and people first, cars second. Europeans regularly vacation by bike, and they can choose from seventeen routes in the EuroVelo network crisscrossing and connecting countries. In the fall of 2023 I biked a five-week section of EuroVelo 6, the "rivers route," taking us from France to Vienna. Because we followed major rivers and canals, the bulk of the route was flat—brilliant! It was signed well for navigation and beautifully designed, taking us each day through a few villages for provisions and to admire ancient churches and village centers before heading back to the river. I highly recommend it; we were charmed daily.

Running Boston as a bandit, 1986.
Josh Levine photo

LESSON 5

Stop doubting yourself, trust your strengths.

You can go the distance
We'll find out in the long run
—Eagles, "The Long Run"

Midway through the first week of our trip, having battled Florida's heat and humidity and headwinds, I climbed into bed at the Sea Scape Motel in Melbourne Beach with a sick dread. My arms and legs were speckled with heat rash and I had chills, but mostly I had a gut sense that the trip was too much for me. I had been tired, thirsty, hungry, and hot for too many days in a row. I recognized the feeling; I'd had it a couple times when I trained for marathons, like when a bad eighteen-mile run would convince me that I was actually an out-of-shape wimp attempting something far beyond me, over my head. But oh god, the embarrassment of having to tell all the people—my friends, coworkers, the dog sitters—that I couldn't make this bike trip after talking about it for months.

Self-doubt has popped up most of my life to whisper in my ear at low points that I'm not all that strong, not that smart, not that fast—anything that I might aspire to be. Submitting a story to a magazine or applying for a big job? Hah, who do you think you are? The voice is loudest when I've pushed myself outside my comfort zone or when I'm simply exhausted, as I was that night at the Sea Scape.

I slept hard that night and we started early the next day. In the cool of the morning, with no headwinds, the miles came easier. Slowly but steadily I built up my comfort and confidence, growing stronger the rest of that first week until I knew I'd be fine.

I never told Dee that I thought I'd have to quit. She has always been an exceptional athlete: high endurance, high energy, ambitious, and confident. On the scale of athleticism from couch potato to elite, I place myself at the midpoint, fairly active but with average accomplishments. Plenty of people are faster and stronger than me, and plenty of people aren't. But when I struggle with self-doubt and compare myself to exceptionally athletic friends like Dee, my self-appraisal can slip a notch or two.

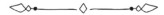

Something was shifting during a few long days of climbing hills in Virginia, nearly midway in our trip. I felt stronger, even physically competent, to a degree I hadn't felt since my forties. With a month of biking under my belt, we had traveled more than 1,200 miles through five states. If I were actually wearing a belt, it would be a little loose, praise be. I was starting to feel like an athlete.

Growing up, athleticism was quietly valued in my family. It was nothing like the soccer-mom travel-team focus you see in young families today. Our parents were much more focused on preparing all five kids to graduate from college and become self-suffi-cient. They noted when any of us had particular skills and interests but never pushed them. My brother, Ron, and sister Linda played tennis pretty well. Mom drove them to tournaments and seemed to enjoy watching their matches. As the youngest, I was always along for the ride. I remember Mom's critique of Ron's tennis at some point was that he was good, he just didn't have "the urge to kill," the competitive drive that would take him to the next level. I was a kid then, but look-ing back now I'm struck by two things: Mom was ac-tually a keen spectator, she wasn't just showing up to the matches; and I can totally relate to not having that fierce, competitive fire that drives so many athletes. Mostly I race against myself.

In high school, I remember Mom driving me some-where and how she dissed a runner at a street corner. Because she didn't stop to let him cross in front of us, he was running in place, waiting for us to pass. "Oh, break your pace," Mom snarled. I was amazed. This woman who didn't know much about running and seemed dismissive of it, how did she even know to use those words? I suspect that if Mom had grown up in a later era, she might have been an athlete—and she definitely would have had the competitive fire. Instead she smoked cigarettes, joined a bowling league, played fierce bridge, and drove us kids to our activities.

Dad was really the first person to teach me, by ex-ample, the restorative power of exercise. Saturday afternoons in Atlanta, after he had mowed our yard in the humid heat, he would stretch out on his back on the floor of our screened porch. Still wearing his thin white V-neck t-shirt damp with sweat, he'd take a quick nap. That was as happy and relaxed as I'd ever seen him. Later in Massachusetts Dad and I would walk up to my high school track together to run and walk laps. I remember the satisfaction of walking home feeling the peace of an honest fatigue.

Taking half-hour runs to blow off stress really kicked in those last few years of high school. I'd be worried about whatever a suburban high schooler worries about—homework, boys, friends, gaining weight. I'd lace up my sneakers and take myself down a few winding bike paths near our house. Breathing hard for a while, I learned, does wonders for clearing out your head and cleaning the slate.

I played on my high school soccer and lacrosse teams but I wasn't any good. I barely knew what I was doing; both sports were new to me. I was timid and the cycle feeds itself. You don't play much because your skills are weak, so your skills never get better. Still, I loved it. I loved the camaraderie of my teammates, loved wearing my red plaid kilt uniform, and loved having something to do every afternoon after school instead of going home. My parents were fighting plenty and toying with divorce. I was counting the days until I left home, first to work at a summer camp on Cape Cod, then off to college.

I kept turning to a run or an afternoon bike ride for stress relief when I got to college. I also tried cigarettes, because my college pal Joan made smoking look so appealing after an afternoon's bike ride. She and I took long rides on the country roads surrounding us at UMass Amherst. I took my first true bike trip with Joan, riding one day from Amherst to her sister's house outside of Hartford, Connecticut. It poured rain most of the way but I loved it.

Meeting Dee in Boston, three years after college, pushed my running and biking to new distances—marathons and hundred-mile century rides—in my twenties. Endurance activities suit me. I have no fast-twitch muscles for speed; my reaction time in sports like pickleball that require coordination is slow. But putting one foot in front of the other, pedaling turn by turn? I can do that. If I can settle into a comfortable pace, I'm happy to run for hours or bike for days. People have praised me for being disciplined, but I'm not. Running, biking, and going for a hike are forms of play to me, activities I enjoy and perfect complements to my sedentary desk work and my tendency to overthink. Out for a run or bike ride, I can daydream or enjoy good conversation while savoring the breeze, the smells, the sights.

And yet I have a hard time calling myself an athlete. What I wrestle with is body image. Peter, a Durham running friend, says an athlete is someone who goes out to run when it's dark, cold, and raining, as he and I have done. But to me, an athlete is lean, with visible muscle definition. I have never in my life been particularly lean. At best I am average, with body fat padding me in places where I wish it didn't.

After running my second Boston Marathon (this time legitimately qualifying for it), a few days after turning forty, I remember assessing myself. It was spring break for the kids so we sent Bob home from Boston to Ohio and the kids and I drove on to Mystic, Connecticut, where we lived when Kate and Tommy were little. We stayed in a hotel, which is not the worst place to come down with a virulent stomach bug (Tommy had been sick on our drive out from Ohio). I flopped around helpless and weak in the hotel bed for a few days while the kids ordered room service and watched TV, happy as clams. When a dear friend came to take the kids to the aquarium, I got up and stood naked in front of the hotel room's full-length mirror. You're forty, I told myself. You just ran a marathon and you haven't eaten for two days. This is probably as lean as you'll get. And it was. The classic middle-age metabolism stuff hit me in my fifties. My belly grows easily, my thighs thicken, my inner arms flap. It doesn't seem to matter that I still run and bike and such.

It's sad to think of how much of my life I've spent unhappy with how my body looks. Meanwhile my body has done whatever I've asked it to do: Grow and birth two babies, run seven marathons, ride my bike for miles. Years ago, a guy in Northeastern University's development office got a surprised look on his face when I told him I was running a marathon that weekend. "It's just," he stammered, "you don't look like a marathoner." He made that comment more than thirty years ago. It's kind of stuck with me.

But a month into my East Coast trip, just when I thought I could never shed weight again, my stomach grew flatter and my legs leaner. If a stranger at a diner or convenience store asked me what I was doing, I finally felt like I looked like someone who was riding her bike on a long-distance trip.

It's not just middle-aged weight that I was losing. With each passing day, I was shedding long-held self-doubt about my strength, my competence, and my ability to sometimes accomplish above-average feats.

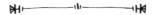

Maine, our final state of the ride, was no piece of cake. The hills along the coast are tough and relentless. We had a gusty headwind and near con-stant hills one day for most of the sixty-two miles. And bridges. I lost count after the fourth big bridge. It started to feel like our last week in Maine and our first week in Florida were strange bookends, testing me physically and emotionally. They shared headwinds and bridges. Florida was miserably hot and the flattest state; Maine was cold and the hilliest state.

There was also something mental at play. In road races of any distance, short or long, I'm often a 90 percenter. I'll be doing just fine, running a respectable pace, until the last 10 or 15 percent of the route. Then mentally I fall apart and want to quit. I once interviewed a fitness coach to write a column about the phenomenon and what to do about it. "You've lost your focus," he told me, "and you won't get it back by trying to force it. Instead, you need to pick a new focus. You could try to pass the three people in front of you, for example." Which, by the way, never worked. If I'm tired at the end of a race, chances are I won't be passing you. My competitive drive is more with myself than with others.

Something like this 90 percent mindset was likely going on during that last week of the ride. There we were in the last 250 or so miles of maybe 2,900 total miles. My head was too focused on the end, which made a tough day of riding into the wind and up hills even tougher.

Back home in Durham after our trip and back at work, I eased my transition back to the real world with my seven-mile bike commute on the American Tobacco Trail (part of the East Coast Greenway) to work. My coworkers welcomed me back warmly and laughed at my stories. One coworker told me that he thought Dee and I set a record for riding the route in fifty-seven days. It was funny to consider, seeing as we rode at such a comfortable pace and enjoyed eight or nine days off with friends and family.

My body still felt strong and capable. My work clothes fit much better post-trip. I tried to keep eating well and moving as much as possible because I didn't want to slide backwards into extra weight. I liked this lighter, stronger version of myself.

Running a marathon isn't very healthy for your body, I often tell people. The training process, at least for me, always felt like just getting accustomed to beating yourself up physically for hours so that when it comes time to run the actual race, your body is like, oh yeah, we're doing this thing for four long hours again. The true lasting benefit of marathons, for me, is a mental one, the metaphor: You can do this hard thing because you've run a marathon. You learn that you can endure. Because I've run 26.2 miles, I know I can meet a deadline for a mammoth work project, endure a long dental procedure, finish a long car trip, and any number of other exhausting and tedious situations.

And yet, grueling as it can be, a marathon only lasts for half a day. Dee and I biked nearly daily for two months up the coast, the longest continuous time I've ever lived that way.

A few weeks after our trip, I brought my bike into Bullseye, my Durham bike shop, for a much needed tune-up after those 3,000 miles. I thought the chain and rear cassette of cog wheels needed to be cleaned and the front derailleur adjusted a bit because the chain was slipping. The mechanic brought out a measuring tool and showed me how the chain links were so worn and stretched they needed to be replaced, along with the rear cassette.

I walked home from the shop feeling a funny pride. I'd never worn down a bike chain before, at least that I knew of. That stretched-out bike chain was my virtual medal. I could stand on a podium and accept it with grace and pride: I am an athlete, badass and all.

Trip planning: The winter before we left, Dee and I went down a list of stops to see where we might know people who could put us up for the night. We ended up with a third of our stays with family and friends, a third in Airbnbs, and a third in motels. Sally Ann Hay photo

Along the Halifax River in Daytona, Florida. Deirdre Bird photo

In Georgetown, South Carolina, our AirBnb host helped me change my rear flat before we left their place in the morning.

Dee documents her first sighting of cotton in a field in North Carolina

*Passing through Washington DC and the National Mall on a quiet
Sunday morning*

*Greeting Dennis, left, and Niles at the East Coast Greenway Alliance
office just off the greenway in Durham, North Carolina*

Touring Cape Cod near Eastham. John Blakeslee photo

Our second to last state-line crossing

Dee on the greenway running through the stunning Scarborough Marsh in Maine

Made it. My tears started here on the edge of town.

Loading Rover on the Amtrak train in Providence, bound for North Carolina. I'm in pjs, hoping to sleep; the porter appropriately wears white gloves.

It was great to see Bob again, of course, but the reunion that made me cry was with two furry friends.

Outside John's bike & surf shop in Florida. I'm smiling because my water bottle is newly filled. Note my long sleeve shirt in the blazing sun and Dee's new riding wear for the heat: the sundress she brought for apres *riding.*

LESSON 6

It's OK to ask for help.

If the sky above you grows dark and full of clouds
And that old north wind begins to blow
Keep your head together and
call my name out loud
Soon you'll hear me knockin' at your door

—Carole King, "You've Got a Friend"

Grit and endurance are great, certainly. But staying safe also feels good. A few weeks before I left work for the bike trip, my coworker Debbie urged me to be sensible about things. Don't be an EDIer, she said: those folks who insist you have to ride Every Damn Inch of the East Coast Greenway to say you completed it. It was wise advice.

On mile sixty-three of a long, hot day of riding into the wind in Florida, day five of our trip, I'd emptied my two water bottles and didn't want to pilfer from Dee's meager supply. The route was all residential; we passed no shops or restaurants for refueling. Finally I spied a bike shop and we pulled into the driveway, beleaguered. The door was locked with a sign saying they'd be right back. Grateful for the shade of the shop's front porch, we milled around a bit. I fantasized about drinking cold water. Soon enough

John, the owner, pulled up in his tall black van. He greeted us and we followed him inside like puppy dogs. I listened to a few of his stories ("ah, Seven Mile Bridge, I like to ride repeats on that in the headwinds") but I was hyper-focused on making sure he filled our water bottles, as he had offered.

I laughed at the title of a book sitting on his counter, *A Really Long Day*. "I know about long days," I said. But he told me the book is a cyclist's story of riding the 4,200-mile Trans Am cross-country race with a short crew and other complications. Translation: Our challenges these last few days in hot sun and wind are nothing compared to this man's struggles and accomplishments. The longer we talked to John, the more like a rookie I felt. He had no interest in our heavy touring bikes, which must look like overloaded elephants to a fast cyclist like him.

Then he told us that he saw us struggling on the road a little earlier.

"John! You could drive ahead of us up to Melbourne Beach and block the wind for us in that big van!" Dee exclaimed, kidding him about the last ten miles of our day. All three of us laugh.

"Hell, I can just throw your bikes on the van and drive you to the motel," he kidded.

We all laughed a bit, *ha ha ha*. Because what losers would do that, right?

As two white, older women, we were aware that we traveled through the South with plenty of privilege. Dressing in running shorts and pastel t-shirts rather than loudly colored cycling gear made us even less threatening.

Our privilege was on full display one hot morning in South Carolina. We were desperate for some shade for a rest stop, so we plopped ourselves on the concrete front porch of a small private school, the only building we'd seen for miles. Dee even helped herself to an electrical outlet on the porch to charge her phone. The headmistress of the Montessori school opened the front door to check us out. We smiled innocently and thanked her for the shade on the hot day. She asked a few questions about the trip, then offered us bathrooms and ice for our water bottles from the teachers' workroom. Would we have been welcomed so warmly if we were two young black men? It's sobering.

Friends and strangers worried about our safety, but we never felt uncomfortable. It would have been different if I was on my own. Few situations scare Dee. In her company, some of that bravery rubs off on me. But I've rarely felt unsafe on a bike trip. There's a visible, non-threatening innocence about a person traveling with just a few possessions and their bike. People tend to show compassion and want to help, like offering cold water and advice on the route.

The winter before our trip I was talking with a carpenter at our river house in rural North Carolina. "Will you be packing?" he asked me. "Yes, I'll have two rear panniers," I told him, a little puzzled. Then I realized that wasn't the kind of packing he meant. Dee and I kept laughing at the thought of tucking little handguns in our handlebar bags. The next time a rude school bus—it's always school buses—drove too close or cut us off with a right turn, we could just whip out our guns and show them who's boss.

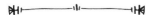

We rode off for North Myrtle Beach, South Carolina, in a steady morning drizzle. The rain got stronger but the sights were distracting as we hit Business 17: seafood restaurants with silly names, streets flooded like crazy along the beachfront in Garden City and Surfside Beach. When we saw a sign announcing we had entered Myrtle Beach, I called out to Dee to pull under the awning in a little shopping strip so I could check our map. I fumbled with the map on my phone because my fingers were too wet to make it work right. The rain got harder so we waited a while, watching puddles grow to flood stage on Business 17. Directly across the highway from us was a Harley Davidson shop. Its parking lot was full of pickup trucks, part of the massive crowds of motorcycle people flocking to the Myrtle Beach area for the annual "bike" week—the other kind of bike.

Remember that day in Florida when we battled heat and headwinds and we stopped at John's surf shop? Dee had kidded him about how he could drive his big black van in front of us for our last miles to block the wind, and he laughed about how he had a bike rack, he could just drive us? *Ha ha ha*, we had all laughed. But Dee and I talked about it the next morning. She surprised me by saying she would have been fine with accepting a ride at that point. Each of us thought the other wouldn't want that. So we clarified a key point: Asking for help is OK.

It's a lesson that's cropped up for me plenty of times as an adult. When I was a young mom with a baby and a toddler in a new town, I learned to seek out women who seemed to parent well and I'd ask if they wanted to hang out. Mom dating, so to speak, because I was desperate for the company of people who understood what my life was like and who could offer grown-up conversation while our kids played. In my fifties, I met my friend Cate at yoga class and learned about her work as a therapist and career coach. I have leaned on her wisdom a bit to get through a few tough job and life situations.

In the Myrtle Beach rains, we started shivering and Dee's lips turned a purplish blue. I knew it was time to seek assistance. We walked into the pawn shop beside us to ask if anyone with a truck could drive us twenty-five miles up the road to our North Myrtle Beach hotel. Two men said they would be glad to help but their trucks were full of stuff. A woman dismissed us. "Sorry, we have to work," she said, with classist undertones that I'd heard a few days earlier in rural South Carolina. I had leaned my bike against a cart of ice bags outside of a convenience store and a delivery guy moved it, saying gruffly, "Some of us have work to do." He caught himself with something like, "You probably worked, too, to earn your time off."

We dashed across the flooded highway to the Bike Week crowd hanging out in clouds of cigarette smoke under the Harley Davidson awning. We tried our truck question again—seeing as the parking lot was full of pickup trucks—only to get weird stares and wise-cracks about how we "need a motor on those things." Drenched and shivering, I looked at the map one more time. We were close to the greenway, I just couldn't see it. We pulled our bikes out past the small lakes growing in the driveway. Dee happened to look left and spotted the nicely paved greenway, hiding behind a big RV parked on the highway shoulder.

We started pedaling madly as the rain came down even harder. Some of the puddles were so deep that my ankles were submerged. All I could do was laugh. Which I did, madly, for blocks. We followed the greenway, happy for the signs guiding us and no traffic stress but getting wetter and colder and hungrier.

As we neared forty-five miles, with fifteen still to go to our motel, we pulled up to a real estate office so we could check the map under an awning. Dee went inside to ask about the nearest coffee shop. The kind women at the front counter invited us in. They offered us their Keurig machine and all the coffee pods we wanted. We dripped water with every step through their lobby. We made coffee. While Dee used the restroom, one of the women asked me if we wanted snacks. I looked at her longingly, feeling like a cold, hungry, homeless child: Yes, please! I was getting better at accepting gifts on this trip. Our needs were so simple yet so urgent.

We stood in the heavily air-conditioned reception area, too wet to sit on their chairs, and inhaled coffee and peanut butter crackers from a big basket of snacks. Dee, eats fairly lightly and loves to share meals and snacks, suggested we share a pack of crackers. I glared at her while helping myself to my own package and devouring all six crackers in no time.

We chatted with the women about real estate and I studied the rest of our route on my phone. It was a series of zigzags crossing Route 17 while trying to avoid that main road. A husband and wife strolled in, real estate clients, and joined our conversation. The husband conferred with me on our route. Finally, with great resolve, Dee and I gathered up our things, took a photo with the nice ladies, and headed back out.

Pulling on our cold, sopping wet rain jackets was painful. Just as we were building up the nerve to climb on our wet seats, the man came out the door and looked at me.

"I know you're probably dead set on finishing your ride, but I have a truck," he said. "We could drive you and the bikes."

I looked past him to Dee, standing about fifteen feet away with her back to me. She whipped her head around and shot a big thumbs up. It was unanimous, then.

Wayne's red pickup truck was big, shiny, and new, but he was fine with loading our wet and gritty bikes in the back. Brenda offered us towels from a tall stack of them that were sitting magically in the cab. The big, plush white towels were perfect for mopping up some of our dripping and for wrapping around us like blankets. While Wayne navigated us to the Hampton Inn, Brenda showed us photos on her phone of her two boys and beautiful grandchildren. Wayne and Brenda were my newest best friends.

The Myrtle Beach monsoon and a few other days aside, we had remarkable luck staying just ahead or behind rainstorms throughout our trip. It's as if we were traveling with a protective shield around us. One day in rural Virginia, for example, we rode all after-noon under a dark sky. We could smell just-fallen rain on the roads, but we stayed dry. The rain didn't let loose on us until we reached the sad but serviceable Nottoway Inn, a true old-fashioned roadside motel serving drivers just off busy I-85.

We took showers in our funky motel room, then dashed through the downpour to a truck stop next door. Imagine Dee's delight: Subway and Dunkin' Donuts, two of her favorites, side by side! We dined at Subway, then repaired to Dunkin' to sip decaf *digestifs*. With nowhere else to go, we camped out there and played on our phones. I was dressed smartly in pajama pants, sneak-ers, and three shirts, two long-sleeved. Dee was in leggings, sneakers (not her trademark sandals), a shirt, scarf, and jacket. The temperature was perfectly fine outside in the rain, but in our little office/camp the air conditioning was freezing cold. The non-stop flow of Memorial Day weekend motorists passing by us easily may have guessed that these two strangely dressed women were homeless. That's sometimes how it feels on a bike trip, that you are homeless and dependent on the kindness of strangers. Instead, we were just two very lucky tourists.

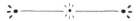

All the nice things that people said about our ride during those two months, about how we had grit and were badass and all, we truly earned on our second to last day of riding. Like our first day so many weeks ago out of Key West, we began the day full of innocence. Our hosts served us a lovely send-off breakfast that included blueberry cake. We waved goodbye wearing a bit of rain gear, thinking the sky might clear. Ha!

Fog and light rain gave way to windy rain, then downpours. The temperature was in the fifties, far colder than Dee and I had clothes for. We stopped after about twenty miles at a diner to warm up and dry off. Over french toast and coffee, I scouted for someone with a pickup truck to take us down the road. An older man sitting at the counter nearby told us about his motorcycle trip long ago and his lobstering work these days. We asked him about a lift, but his car couldn't carry bikes. We rode on in heavy rain another five to ten miles, checking once at a convenience store for anyone who might give us a ride. Mostly the other customers and store clerk just stared at us flatly: Dee in her bright yellow rain poncho, me in my florescent pink windbreaker, both of us dripping wet.

The rain lightened for a bit and we refocused on riding. When the route took us down a dirt road with enormous puddles and muddy gullies, we just had to belly laugh. Riding this road in the pouring rain was gritty, no question.

Fifteen miles from our destination, we came to another diner in an otherwise tiny crossroads of a town. Guessing we wouldn't have much to choose from for dinner where we were headed, we stopped. We sat shivering and dripping and consumed endless cups of coffee and odd snacks: French fries and apple pie. Meanwhile the rain and wind picked up outside. We tried the truck question again with two guys seated near us. One guy told us he was driving a Jaguar that he smashed into a deer; it can't fit two bikes. He offered to text his boss to ask about borrowing his truck, just down the road, but that option seemed to fizzle out. "I'm fighting with three lawyers right now who are all trying to steal my money," the young man explained.

Our issues weren't quite so complicated. We pulled on our wet outer layers and headed back out on the road. I actually hoped for hills to climb so I could warm up as the rain poured and the wind blew. Some of the gusts felt strong enough to blow me into the lane of traffic, so it took all my focus to ride steadily and straight ahead. The night before I had watched a short video circulating on social media of Paul McCartney playing a surprise, pop-up concert in a bar. I started singing "Let It Be" to myself. Like the *inch by inch, row by row* song that got me across Seven Mile Bridge in the Florida Keys, I realized I didn't know most of the words to "Let It Be" anymore. Fragments, including *whisper words of wisdom, let it be*, sufficed.

We got a kind, sympathetic greeting from the proprietors as we dripped our way into the Blueberry Patch Motel office. "On a day like this," the man told us, shaking his head, "I would have picked you two up in my truck if I had passed you."

At a scenic overlook before we crossed the Penobscot Narrows Bridge at Fort Knox in Prospect, Maine. My smile is fake.

LESSON 7

Just cross the bridge; they aren't all scary.

You gain strength, courage, and confidence by every experience in which you really stop to look fear in the face. You are able to say to yourself, 'I lived through this horror. I can take the next thing that comes along.'
— Eleanor Roosevelt

*I've got many rivers to cross
But I can't seem to find my way over*
—Jimmy Cliff, "Many Rivers to Cross"

Making your way up the Atlantic coast of Florida by bike means crossing back and forth over the Intracoastal Waterway some five hundred and forty seven times, or so it seems. Most of the bridges are flat and low, not scary and high. But still it felt like immersion therapy for my bridge phobia.

I used to love bridges. They take you to fun places, after all, like islands and beaches. I trace my fear back to a night in my early forties when I was on a road trip to Green Bay with my Ohio pals to run a marathon. I took my turn driving around midnight, a time when I don't belong doing anything functional. Lightning cracked the sky and I was driving on a highway overpass bridge under construction in Chicago. I felt overpowered by Patrice's huge SUV. I could see how easy it would be to crash through the jersey barriers on either side of the lane, sending us all free-falling to our deaths.

I've since read that a similar eroding of balance, or equilibrium, is fairly common among women after childbirth. I see it as some kind of alchemy of hormones and responsibility and fatigue. Maybe. All I know is sharp drop-offs suddenly gave me the willies, a fear that I can feel through my whole body. On a bicycle, nice flat bridges are fine. But bridges that gain altitude and have low or open railings give me cold sweats and a dull dread in my gut, no matter how much I tell myself it's silly.

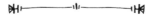

Four of us—me, Dee, and two friends riding with us for a few days—were approaching Cape Cod on a late morning in June. When New Englanders plan a trip to the Cape, they always have to factor in what time of day they'll be driving and what that means for bridge traffic. The Sagamore Bridge, crossing the Cape Cod Canal from the mainland to the Cape, is only two lanes each way and clogs easily.

Cyclists are required to walk our bikes across the Sagamore, I was happy to learn. But even walking is unsettling. We were on a raised, narrow sidewalk, about a foot higher than the bridge deck and maybe three feet wide. We walked facing the trucks and cars heading off the Cape. It was loud and unnerving and very open-air, with a bit of a headwind. Dee walked at the head of our group. Completely unfazed, she raised her phone overhead to take selfies of our group. Later we saw the photos: Poyee, Mark, and I all had our heads down, looking grim. I was telling myself reassuring things about how at least the sidewalk is solid cement, not open grating.

Actually, I got a little teary as we crossed the Sagamore. It was less challenging to walk across the bridge than it would have been to ride across it, balanced on two wheels while imagining how easily I could fall off the edge. I thought back to our first day of biking over Seven Mile Bridge. We had come so far—roughly 2,300 miles— and seen so much. The green and slightly delirious cyclist I was that day in Florida felt seasoned, stronger and more grounded about challenges like headwinds and bridges. Our quiet march across the bridge (it was too loud for conversation, anyway) offered me a little time to appreciate those changes and lessons learned.

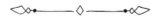

Dee has been kindly patient with my bridge phobia over the years, even though she can't relate. I keep trying to make light of it. Quickly I brought my bike, Rover, into the issue, letting him speak for me.

"Rover didn't like that," I'd tell Dee, after we'd bike over some high bridge with a gap between the railing and the bridge surface, a gap big enough that I could picture a bike wheel slipping off the edge.

On the day we crossed from New Hampshire into Maine, Tom—a cyclist who completed the East Coast Greenway a month ahead of us—rode with us. Sitting beside me on a rest break, he swiped through his trip photos on his phone to show me a few highlights of what was ahead, including the distinctive lines of the Penobscot Narrows Bridge at Fort Knox. It looked enormous. The way Tom shook his head and didn't say much else frightened me even more. I'm not sure if it's better to know in advance or to just happen upon a big bridge. For our next few days, every time we took a turn and saw water, I wondered if that bridge was coming up. So much for living in the moment and enjoying the journey!

Cyclists know about the optical illusion that happens on the road. Hills get distorted. What can look like a monster climb from afar turns out to be not so steep when you finally get to it. It usually happens when you're on top of a hill, looking downhill and then back up the other side. We started to see the Fort Knox bridge supports way in advance of reaching it. We stopped at a scenic overlook, a pull-off where you can park your car or RV and get a good look at the bridge and the Penobscot River far below. I couldn't even bring myself to walk closer to the scenic overlook plaza. Dee started to take photos. These are my least favorite photos, me faking a smile while feeling sick in my gut. A fellow who had just parked his big pick-up at the overlook offered to take a photo of us together. We started the familiar small talk. I knew Dee and I were thinking the same thing: He could drive me and my bike across the bridge. *Ha ha ha*, we laughed as we suggested this to him. But he didn't bite, and I was ready to get the bridge over with.

I've witnessed enough friends and family members dealing with trauma-related issues to know that a balanced approach to handling my fear makes sense to me. I want to silence, ignore, or laugh at the thought patterns that kick in when I'm faced with edges and steep drop-offs. Thinking about how easy it would be to fall over the railing is silly, I tell myself. But that's where my mind goes, picturing what the plunge down to the icy cold Penobscot River, for example, would feel like. The butterflies in my gut and my quickening heartbeat are real. So I aim for a balance of not indulging the fear too much but acknowledging it's there. What that looks like, what Dee and Bob and others have come to recognize, is me growing quiet. No silly chatter, no admiring the view, just a steady focus a few feet ahead of me. Which is fine when a bridge span takes just a few minutes to cross. Thinking back to Seven Mile Bridge, riding on it for an hour in headwinds, I'm not surprised I grew delirious. That's a long time to hold a mental balance.

As you approach the Fort Knox bridge, you have the choice to go up an elevator to its observation tower (hell no). You have to take an exit ramp down a hill to reach the tower entrance. Dee considered that option but decided against the extra hill work. I told her to go on across the bridge, that I'd cross slowly. I might let myself walk. But it turns out the bridge isn't really that bad. It's actually kind of small, one lane each way with a decent shoulder. It's just the tall supports that made it look so daunting. With light traffic around me, I started out walking, but halfway across I told myself

it was silly. I hopped on my bike and started pedaling.
I was grinning by the time I neared solid ground.

Dee had used her waiting time to find bushes for a
quick wee on the other side. She was disappointed that
she had missed capturing my victorious ride on camera.

"You conquered it!" she called out, proudly.

"I wouldn't exactly call it conquering," I told her. "But
I crossed it."

*No one was home when we visited the split-level in Lutherville,
Maryland, where I lived during junior high school.*

LESSON 8

Connect the dots by visiting your past.

There are places I'll remember
All my life, though some have changed
Some forever, not for better
Some have gone and some remain
—John Lennon and Paul McCartney,
"In My Life"

Ron and Adrienne, my brother and sister-in-law, picked us up at Fort Fisher on the Cape Fear River to save us the last ten miles or so of our ride to their house in Wilmington, North Carolina. I felt a rush of comfort at seeing them pull into the ferry parking lot. They had a nice, sturdy rack for our bikes. I was happy to slide into their comfy SUV and watch the road go by from the backseat. We were driving on the busy beach roads that we would have had to navigate to get to their place.

They took us to dinner on the riverfront in downtown Wilmington. It was a beautiful evening. I ordered seafood and a glass of wine, two things I hadn't had yet on the trip. We talked about family and familiar things. Ron is a guy of few words, like our father was. But he told me more at dinner than he ever has about how he was feeling during Mom's decline. In her early days of dementia she became paranoid about him stealing her money, after a few years of my sister Bar-

bara and Ron helping Mom with her financial paper-
work and other things. As the only boy in the family,
Ron had long escaped Mom's running critique that we
four sisters knew too well. She'd assess our looks, our
relationships, our kids, our homes. She would find our
weak spots and pick at them, painfully. In her com-
promised state, Mom turned on Ron. I'm sure it left
him reeling.

I was glad to talk about those days in a relaxed setting, watching the sun sink down over the river. Back
when Mom was slipping, we siblings were all piecing
together bits of information from a distance. Our communication got frazzled, our emails misinterpreted.
We've had to build back trust in each other over the
years. Here at sunset along the Cape Fear River, Ron
helped me close the book on much of that time.

In some ways on the bike trip with Dee, I fell back into
a familiar little sister role. I had some kind of unspo-
ken understanding that her needs were more important because I am younger. It's nothing that Dee did;
it's my years of training as the youngest kid. Whatever
was going on with my three sisters—high school concerns, then college concerns, then job and relationship
concerns—carried far more weight than what was going on with Ron and me, the babies. Even Ron, a year
and a half older than me, led a more important life as
he started playing Little League and tournament tennis. I was just tagging along, keeping quiet and hoping
Mom or Dad would give me money for the snack bar.

With Dee, this role manifested most often in our
nightly bed choices. When we got to someone's home

where there's just one bed and a couch, like at my brother's house, I immediately claimed the couch. Dee has always been a terrible sleeper. Her chances of getting some sleep are better if she's at least on a real bed. I am generally an ace sleeper and comfortable on most flat surfaces. Give me a blanket and pillow and I'm cozy. We had shared a couple motel beds so far, but being in separate rooms was better. That way if either of us woke up in the middle of the night, we were able to read a bit, check emails and such and hopefully fall back to sleep without waking up the other person.

After a fun day off, Ron and Adrienne sent us off from their driveway. As Dee took a quick tour with Adrienne of her garden, Ron asked me, "So, has the trip lived up to your expectations so far?"

I had to smile. It's just the kind of question our dad would have asked. This must be what semi-retirement has done for my brother, I thought. He seemed more aware and thoughtful.

"Yes," I assured him. "I'm having a blast."

One rainy evening in a dreary Baltimore hotel room, I studied the East Coast Greenway map and gasped. Just a mile or so from our route was the Lutherville neighborhood where I lived during junior high and a year of high school. Dee indulged me and agreed to add a few miles so I could travel down Memory

Lane. The extra miles were hilly, so I felt guilty. But I also got excited as I started to spot familiar street names: Greenspring, Seminary Ridge, Tally Ho. We turned into my old subdivision, a late 1960s community plopped down on a former horse farm. Amazingly, after forty-four years the houses looked the same. The suburban colonials and split-levels hadn't morphed into McMansions, and they weren't neglected. It was surreal to be there.

The best thing: The gravel bike path that ran behind our house, once the carriage lane to an old farmhouse, was still there, now paved. In those awkward junior high years, that path was my escape route from unhappy parents and my awkward life. I'd jump on my baby blue Schwinn and be free. It's funny to realize that path was my first greenway.

While I was losing myself to remembered angst and escape, Dee was fascinated to learn that I lived in such a classically suburban setting. Our 1970s split-level looked pretty much the same. The owners had added a screened sunroom where our back patio was. No one was home, so I sat on the front steps and, very out of character, asked Dee to take my photo. I sent the photo with "Guess where I am?" to Barbara and Ron, my siblings who also lived there. Sandy and Linda were out of college by then.

"Wow," Barbara texted back, appropriately. Ah, what she and I endured there. We had moved from Atlanta and started in new schools. We watched Mom and Dad fight more regularly. We spent many hours in the downstairs den, complete with 1970s multi-colored shag carpeting, listening to albums and losing ourselves in books.

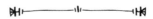

We left New York City on a Monday morning and stopped at a deli in Port Chester, New York, for lunch. Dee was reuniting with a friend from thirty years ago during her year of teaching in Armenia. I got to see Jodi, a friend from Echo Hill Camp on the Chesapeake Bay. We hadn't seen each other since we were fifteen-year-old counselors-in-training more than forty years ago. We'd been in touch a tiny bit on Facebook. She reached out to ask if my trip would bring us anywhere near where she lives in Harrison—and there we were.

Jodi spied me through the window of the deli as Dee and I locked our bikes outside. She ran out to give me a hug and said the nicest thing I can imagine hearing, at fifty-eight, from a friend who knew me as a young teen: "You haven't changed a bit!" Jodi, meanwhile, was beautiful, a glamorous version of the bunkmate I remember in alligator shirts and painter's pants. She is a graphic designer and is married with two teenage boys. All through lunch I couldn't get over what a kick it was to see her.

Those two camp summers on the Chesapeake Bay were quick for me but pivotal. I was an unhappy junior high kid, but at Echo Hill I met peers who felt like my people. I learned to sail, which was why I had talked my parents into letting me go. I learned to love the Quaker traditions at the root of the camp's founding, honoring quiet and respect and the natural world. I fell into deep crushes on two Venezuelan brothers who played guitar and sang Neil Young and Crosby, Stills & Nash. Those summers helped set my compass, teaching me I would find people like me and passions to pursue no matter how much of a misfit I felt I was in school. Seeing Jodi brought some of that long-ago time back to me.

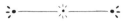

A runner stopped to talk with us at a little beach park in southern Connecticut where Dee and I had set out a picnic. The runner had a familiar New England accent, a familiar look about his weathered face and wiry frame, and he knew some of the road races I used to run when we lived in Mystic, Connecticut, just up the road.

We were definitely getting close to so many New England memories. I want to say my New England "roots," but that's tricky. I've lived in so many places, which ones can I claim have offered me roots? I was born in Cleveland, but we moved when I was three to Atlanta. We left Atlanta for Baltimore as I started seventh grade, then to Boston's suburbs as I started 11th grade. Sometimes I envy people who have grown up in one place, surrounded by extended family and their own history. As a child of the suburbs, I mostly know about sub-developments and driving five miles to go to the grocery store.

Something clicked for me when we moved to Boston in high school; it felt like coming home. Boston's suburbs are small towns, each with character and town centers. Ours had a town pond where I taught sailing one summer. I went to college in western Massachusetts and spent most of my twenties in Boston. It's the city and region where I came of age. Each day that we ride closer to Boston feels like coming home. But I loved my home in North Carolina, too. How do you pick one home if you've loved many?

We biked across the tiny state of Rhode Island in one day, mostly in the rain. Of our fifty-eight miles, more than twenty-five were on greenways, older paths that Rhode Island built decades ago. It made for easy, pleasant riding despite the cool rain. For two hours we didn't worry about traffic or navigation.

I love Rhode Island as another of my former homes. I landed my first job out of college here at the U.S. Yacht Racing Union in Newport. Back then I rode bikes to work with my coworker and housemate, also a new college graduate. His boss led the three of us on some gorgeous bike rides on Aquidneck Island, the large island with Newport at its tip. We'd roll along quiet back roads and then along the water, with strips of beach and rocks and views of the bay and river.

I left for Boston after a year or so, but four years later I circled back to Providence to help start *Rhode Island*

Monthly magazine. I was a newlywed. For a year Bob and I juggled living between Boston and Providence. He had a good job as an assistant athletic director at Harvard; I was excited to work on a "real," not alumni, magazine. It was part of my job to explore the Ocean State, so on weekends Bob and I drove around the state to try restaurants and visit towns.

Later, raising young kids in Mystic, Connecticut, we started spending a week each summer in Rhode Island, renting little houses at the beach even though it was just twenty miles or so from our home. Those beach towns have a down-to-earth, undiscovered feel. They are where locals head for vacation, not where out-of-state tourists flock. Eventually, after we moved to Ohio, we bought a place near the beach in Misquamicut, Rhode Island. We rented it out through the summers, saving a week or two each year for ourselves. We wanted the kids, growing up in Ohio, to remember what the ocean looks like and to stay in touch with our friends from Mystic and Boston. We sold that house after we moved to North Carolina because the drive was too far. But our family still treasures memories of our Misquamicut years.

At a few road and bridge crossings Dee and I caught glimpses of handsome old brick mills that once dominated most of these small towns, physically and financially. You don't find much pretension in Rhode Island. It reminds me of Ohio in that way, down to earth and real, not fancy. Yet we were riding on miles and miles of beautiful greenway. Even in the cool drizzle, I felt my Ocean State love.

From Dee and Sally's house in Lincoln, Rhode Island, we biked down half of the East Bay Bike Path and kept heading east, bound for Cape Cod. Mark, a friend from college who lives outside of Boston, rode with us the next four days along with Poyee, a friend of Dee's. Of all the stretches of our trip, this was the one most peppered with memories — from high school, college, and my early twenties. I was happy to have Mark along to share in the revisiting. His memory is stronger than mine. As we pedaled, he helped fill in some of the blanks of people, places, and stories.

Joan, my UMass pal who introduced me to Mark, grew up in New Bedford, Massachusetts, near where we were headed that day. Mark and I remember visiting Joan's house when we were in college and the fun of getting lost in the swirl of her family of nine siblings. In our senior year at UMass, I started dating a friend of Joan's who was also from New Bedford. After graduation I took a job in Newport, Rhode Island, and drove many weekends from Newport through Fall River to New Bedford and back. Those first few years after college are so much water under the bridge, as the saying goes. I sorted out so much angst and uncertainty about career and love and the future as I steered my big old Chevy Malibu on those weekend drives. Remembering this time, I felt grateful to be on my bike in the company of good friends, my life far more grounded.

That night we stayed with Mary, one of Joan's sisters, and her husband, Peter. They drove us into New Bedford for dinner. As we told stories over our meals, I learned that it was actually Peter's connection, through Joan, that helped me land my first job out of college at the U.S. Yacht Racing Union. I had hoped to connect some dots on my trip, but I hadn't seen this one coming. I raised my mug of the local IPA and toasted Peter with a much belated thanks.

From Provincetown on the far end of Cape Cod we rode a high-speed ferry, ninety minutes to Boston. I sat out on the front deck for the last half hour so I could take in the sights and sounds of Boston Harbor: the islands, a fishing boat, a few sailboats and a big schooner, another ferry, and planes landing at Logan Airport. The transition from the quiet of the Cape to the bustle of a city nearly overwhelmed me.

Boston isn't just any city—it's my city. At least that's how it felt in my twenties when I lived, worked, and played there. I was excited to see it again, up close and personal from my bike seat as we rode to Mark's house.

The ferry pulled into the pier area, which has been built up in recent years. Mark led us deftly through noontime weekday traffic up to Boston Common and down to the Esplanade to pick up the Charles River Bike Path. People were everywhere—office workers on lunch break and tourists visiting downtown. Biking there on a gorgeous day truly blew me away. This is where Dee and I ran at lunchtime thirty-five years ago and where we trained on weekends for our first marathon. This is where I walked and ran with Bob as we started dating, and where I pushed Kate in a baby stroller when she was just a few weeks old.

We biked along the Charles River to Harvard Square, also a familiar playground for each of us over the years. Bob worked at Harvard years ago and Mark's wife Laurie worked there at the time. Back in the day, Dee and I visited the square often, including dinners of spinach croissants and coffee at Au Bon Pain before a concert or movie. That day, we ate a perfect lunch of salads and lemonade in the shade at a little park and rode on to Mark's house in Belmont.

Total miles traveled by bike that day: thirty-seven. Years, decades, life phases revisited: too many to count.

Bob came to Boston for our last rest day. That night we headed to a party at Jessica's house. Jessica is a former colleague from my days working at North-eastern University. She offered to host a reunion with as many of our former communications office cowork-ers as she could track down. Dee remembered many of these friends, although it has been decades since she'd seen them. She was the business professor who I met for noontime runs and who sometimes joined us after hours for concerts.

These were the friends who knew me when I was developing my crush on That Guy Bob down the hall from us and cheered for our budding relationship. It

Northeastern University employees reunited (from left): Dee, Chris, Karen, Josh, Kelly, Jessica, me, Bob

was a wonderful workplace. Looking back on those years, I see we were a remarkable team. Karen edited the faculty/staff newspaper while I edited the alumni magazine. We had four or five writers, including Jessica, working beats for our publications and the media. Kelly worked as our administrative assistant, vibrant and funny and sharp. We worked closely with the photo department, run by Josh. We were single twenty-somethings in Boston and we made the most of it, going out to dinners and concerts and movies together.

Seeing so many of these friends again was wonderful. Jessica, our host, has married Phil, a kind and handsome guy. She teaches writing at Emerson University and has published an astounding nine novels so far. Karen was there with her husband, Dan. I cheered on their relationship, too, during our Northeastern days. Josh was there with his wife, Judi. Chris was a great surprise—I hadn't seen our supportive, good-natured boss in thirty years or so.

Seeing Kelly was another big surprise. I remember hearing that she had moved from Boston to Alaska, married, and moved to Maine. It turns out she's living now on Boston's North Shore; Jessica tracked her down. She was as funny and upbeat as ever. She brought a bottle of champagne that added great festivity to our night. We did a round of toasts but I wasn't feeling terribly articulate, so Bob stepped in for me to thank everyone.

"That Wattsky, she just sets a goal and goes after it," Kelly announced. Her words stopped me. That's not how I think of myself, all directed and confident. But looking through Kelly's lens, I see that I wanted to edit a magazine, check. I chased after That Guy Bob, check. This bike trip, check. Maybe I'm more driven than I realize.

Dee told me the next day as we biked out of Boston that she had enjoyed watching me laugh so heartily with my old friends. The laughs came so easily; my memories are so rich of those years. Heading north, I savored the feeling of integrating my life's eras, of shaking off some of the dust on my brain's storage files.

I was grateful to Jessica for collecting so many of us and hosting us so graciously. Old friends are the best. They don't have to ask questions like, "What's your favorite state so far?" Instead they wanted to know what I'm eating, if I'm happy, and how my kids are, then they started talking about some funny time way back when. I didn't remember all the stories but I loved the laughs. I felt nicely integrated, my present reconnected with my past, and very grateful.

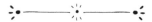

Dee and I stood at the hotel desk in downtown Portsmouth, New Hampshire, where I had to haggle over our room fee. I booked a room for the wrong night; our room that night would be twice as expensive, $400 plus. We hardly felt like riding another five miles or so to a cheaper hotel, and we'd lose the cost of the night I reserved anyway. I felt stupid and discouraged. But when I turned from the counter, I saw my sister Barbara behind me. She had driven two hours from her home in New Hampshire to take us to dinner. She had no idea how seeing her lifted my spirits. Dee had to endure a few hours of sister time and what my mom called our "giggle fests." Barbara's quick, wry sense of humor does it to me every time. She told me that she agreed with Bob's assessment of my blog reports of the trip: We've had too many beautiful days and we've encountered too many nice people. So it's appropriate that day was cloudy and cool. Maybe the next day, as we crossed into Maine, we'd meet some cranky people and find some trashy roads. You never know.

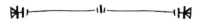

Six years since our bike trip, I still gaze sometimes at a map I've pinned on my bulletin board. On a grayed out view of the East Coast, the greenway's route from Key West to Canada is outlined, with pin-points for the bigger cities it passes through. I feel pride, recognition, and an odd sense of connection studying the map. The route was my home for two months, certainly. But it also tells the basic outline of my life: moving north from Atlanta to Baltimore to Boston. After ten years in Ohio, Bob and I lived in North Carolina for almost twenty years, with plenty of visits to Rhode Island sprinkled in there. Both places claim beautiful stretches of the East Coast Greenway. We've just made a decision to move to Rhode Island permanently, bucking the normal retirement flow to the South. But with so many connections here, I'm sure I'll be seeing North Carolina plenty.

Maybe I can't call one place home because I've been lucky to love so many places and meet dear friends in each one of them. Maybe my home is bigger than one city.

In my Northeastern University office, circa 1987, where I edited the alumni magazine

LESSON 9

Let go of professional ambition as you wrap up your career.

I arise in the morning torn between a desire to improve the world and a desire to enjoy the world. This makes it hard to plan the day.
—E.B. White

O n our longer, more monotonous days of pedaling, I spent some time thinking about my work. Over the years I have focused plenty of energy on my career as an editor and writer. Job after job I've proved myself by beating deadlines and pushing my creativity. As soon as I got bored—the kiss of death for me—or sensed some dysfunction in an organization, I changed jobs and had to prove myself all over again.

From the perspective of nearly a month removed from work and an office, it all seemed a little silly. I'd been building some imaginary portfolio of all my work over the years, desperate to prove my competence. Look at this story, this magazine issue, this website I made! All of that mattered years ago when I needed to win the next new job. So many years of pedaling uphill, churning and churning. Maybe I'd finally reached the end of that climbing. Maybe it's OK to coast, to let the wheels just spin a bit and enjoy the momentum I've built.

I enjoyed dinner visits with both of our kids during our two-day stay in New York City. After dinner with Tommy in Brooklyn, a light drizzle turned to rain. Tommy walked me to a subway station and pointed me to the uptown train. I didn't want to just hang around our hotel room so early in the evening, so I got off the train a few stops early. The rain had tapered off enough that I could walk. On a whim I called Brigitte, a dear friend back in North Carolina. I loved catching up with her as I walked the city blocks.

After we said goodbye I walked a few more blocks and spotted a Dunkin' Donuts. Inside, sitting at a counter facing out to the street, I pulled out a pen and paper to catch up on the last couple of days in New York City for my blog. It felt far different from sitting on a motel bed and writing nightly blog posts while Dee sat on her bed and tried to observe quiet time. It also felt strangely familiar, taking me back four decades to my college days, when I sat in coffee shops and wrote in my journal. Back then, my scribblings were full of longing and questions and goals. I wanted to be in love; I wanted to like myself. I hoped I would land a job doing what I loved, writing.

As I sat watching New Yorkers out the window, I thought about my grown kids (how did that happen?) and how proud they make me feel. I thought of my dear friends, especially all those who were cheering me on via social media. I thought about having the freedom to take this grand adventure. Gratitude washed over me as I realized that so much of the longing of my early twenties has been resolved along the way these last few decades. With so much hard pedaling behind me, I need to do a better job of enjoying life's ride.

Profound thoughts continued throughout our stay in the Big Apple. Dee, Virginia and I attended a Sunday morning Unitarian Universalist church service a few blocks from our hotel. The sermon was about loving a dying world, how to have hope in the face of environmental destruction. I was in tears by the end of the service because the messages were all so relevant: how to find religion in the great outdoors, how to follow our passions as the best defense against cynicism and despair. Through the readings and songs and the minister's message, one lesson hit me most powerfully. Returning home didn't have to mean my life had to return to "normal." If I was intent on understanding and not doubting myself, the journey could continue. Pursuing dreams and embracing opportunities could become more the way I live my life. It was an incredibly hopeful message, helping me to see that the trip's end wasn't necessarily a finish line.

The next morning I stood on the sidewalk outside our Upper West Side hotel and watched the flow of people. It was Monday so they hurried by, heading back to school and work, their faces serious. Savor this moment, I told myself. You get to take a bike ride today. The day of the week didn't matter. I had no meetings, no agendas, no deadlines. How many times, caught up in my work-a-day routine, have I dreamed of blowing it all off and going out to play?

Ten days later Bob flew to Boston for our last rest day of the trip, at Mark and Laurie's house. Mark loaned us his car. As Bob drove me to get a haircut, I asked him how he would feel if I were to cut back my work hours in the near future, to maybe three-fifths or half time. I'd been inspired by so many people I'd met on the trip, from Airbnb hosts to cyclist friends in Connecticut, who are 60-plus and enjoying their free time with active pursuits. I wanted to speed up the timetable for phasing out my work.

"That's fine," he said, staring straight ahead as he drove. "We just have to figure out how to make up that lost income."

I stared straight ahead, too, letting his response register. I expected him to be more encouraging, like everyone else has been on this trip. I sorted out his response, remembering that Bob always worries about money. Having been raised with not much, he is a saver by habit. And retirement isn't anything that calls to him.

I watched Mark and Laurie. They are my age, on the cusp of sixty. Mark worked for the federal government for thirty years. His longest stretch was in a high-stress role with the IRS, one that includes mandatory retirement at fifty-five because of the stress. Meanwhile Laurie, professionally driven for as long as I have known her, continues to work in development. I've been quizzing Mark these last few years about how it feels to have one spouse working, one spouse retired. Is Laurie jealous of his free time? Does he have to do all the errands because he's home? When will she retire?

Everyone's decisions about retirement are as individual as the people themselves. There are so many factors to consider: lifestyle, ambition, dreams, savings, debts. And outlook. I keep seeing retirement as the big prize at the end of four decades of work. After giving all that time to employers, finally my time will be my own. Doesn't everyone crave that? But maybe it's like the idea of working from home. I used to imagine it would be the ultimate luxury to work at home in my pajamas, my loving pups at my side and my schedule fairly flexible. Before the COVID-19 pandemic hit and we all learned to adjust to remote work, I had a couple stretches of working only from home that sometimes made me feel I was going crazy, paranoid when no one returned my emails and guilty when I snuck in a few household chores. Maybe retirement feels like that, more like a loss of structure and interpersonal contact than the gift of freedom. Maybe the grass is always greener, however we spend our days?

I'm in a privileged place to be able to toss these questions around, I know. A few years ago, desperate for a haircut, I tried a new hair salon. My young hairdresser was detailing all the compromises she had to make with her boyfriend about where to live—Chicago or North Carolina?—and when they could move. Trying to be kind and relate to her, I told her how Bob and I will face the same kinds of compromises around retirement. We'll have to figure out how to balance living quietly and simply (my preference) with time living a more urban life (Bob's preference).

"Retirement," she told me, "is a luxury." Ouch.

She's my former hairdresser, by the way. She was even more outspoken about how I needed to up my beauty game. She scolded me that I should wear makeup and get my nails done along with getting better haircuts and some highlights. I bought some lip gloss but I also found a new salon.

Back home in North Carolina after my trip, it was the best of summer, not too hot or humid yet. I found myself paying keen attention to my senses—how the air smells, how a breeze feels, how good coffee tastes— with a focus that I didn't remember before the bike trip. Dee and I enjoyed fifty-seven long days outdoors in all kinds of weather. That time seemed to sharpen my senses. How many times, if ever, as an adult do we get to spend weeks upon weeks outdoors all day?

My head and body crave it. When I used to leave the office on a beautiful day, in all four seasons, I'd think what a waste it had been to spend so many of the daylight hours inside. Chances are good I saw the early sun on a morning run, and I'd be walking the dogs close to sunset when I got home. But all those hours in between! I've felt this pull all my working life. With each new season and a sunny day, I feel like a little kid who can't concentrate in school, who wants to bust out the door and go play.

It was easier in those first few months after the trip to blow off the silly stuff, to not fixate on small disappointments or frustrations. It also made me a little spacy. I'd miss something someone was saying because I was paying attention to the breeze, or a song. Or maybe I was just floating in a slightly surreal bubble, my body and mind still processing what those two months on the road meant. For weeks I dreamed almost every night that Dee and I were still riding. In one dream, someone found an opening in Canada so we agreed to ride on to the North Pole. What puzzled me was that we were sleeping in yet another Airbnb that I couldn't remember checking into. Many nights I woke up to use the bathroom and I couldn't remember where I was—the result of sleeping in fifty or more new places, night after night for weeks.

One day I met a thoughtful friend and fellow communications veteran for coffee. We talked mostly about work stuff. But he wanted to hear a bit about my trip. I stumbled with the usual awkward attempts to sum up two very full months in a few sentences. He asked me, "What did you learn about America?" Wow, I told him. Nobody had asked me that question.

The truth is, I didn't really set out on my bike for two months to learn about America. Call it introspection or navel gazing, but mostly I wanted to learn about me. I wanted to experience the East Coast, no question, but I was really searching for a better understanding of who I am and what I can do.

Right now, I feel no urge to pedal that hard again, literally and figuratively. I'm proud of much that I've accomplished in my work. But I've been keeping score, trying to prove to someone, or myself, that I'm really good at my work. Now I don't feel a need to prove anything. Maybe accomplishing something big outside of a job helped me see that work is something I do, not who I am. I have this feeling of riding up high in a hot-air balloon, floating over my career: I've gained distance, a remove. By letting go of professional ambition, I feel lighter, with a more expansive perspective.

A true role model: Dee's mum at 89, doing yoga in her yard in southern England

LESSON 10

Reframe how you see and talk about aging.

Aging is just another word for living.
—Cindy Joseph

For the last few years I have worked half-time as communications director for the Gerontology Institute at UMass Boston. I've learned a lot about the field of aging studies. Gerontology is the policy and advocacy around aging, not the health and medical science of aging, which is geriatrics. In the gerontology world we talk a lot about ageism and reframing aging to eliminate the stereotypes around growing frail and inept. In theory, I get it. But I remember taking part in a webinar in my first year on the job. As the facilitator waited for everyone to join the Zoom session, she asked us to write in the chat box the first word that came to mind when we thought about aging. "Decline," I answered, knowing it was politically incorrect but an honest reflection of my knees growing cranky, my eyesight diminishing, and other physical weakening.

Reversing that downhill thinking takes work. But I absolutely champion the idea that this time of life, our sixties and older, life's third act, is the best phase of life. We have accumulated wisdom to make better choices. With our eventual destiny closer on the horizon, we tend to waste less time; our days are numbered. As we head towards and begin retirement, many of us have more time and resources. And at least for another decade or so, most of us are reasonably healthy.

Dee, with her nine years on me, has things to teach me about accepting aging gracefully. The day on our trip when we crossed from New Hampshire into Maine, we were joined by a friend Tom and his young friend Maej, a former coworker who was visiting the U.S. for a few months. Maej gamely joined us in hiking boots and rode a borrowed bike, for the first time, in traffic. When we stopped at a Dunkin Donuts after fifteen miles, Maej wisely called it quits. Friends of Dee's gave her and Tom a ride back to Portsmouth.

Another few hours up the road, Tom and Maej surprised us on part of the Eastern Trail, a twenty-mile stretch of crushed stone paths and sidewalks. On the trail Maej was all smiles, riding on flat terrain without traffic. As we said our second goodbyes, she asked Tom to take her photo with us. We were her new role models, she told us.

It's the kind of compliment I try to take kindly when what I really hear is, *I love that you are doing this when you are so old*. Dee and I talked about it as we pedaled on north. People, young women especially, often say these kinds of things to her. She has learned to accept them graciously without making a fuss. Aging well, I realize, includes accepting kind comments that we are, in fact, doing it well.

With Brigitte at a Lions Club ride in rural North Carolina, 2011. Dan Routh photo

LESSON 11

Hug your friends.

And it never feels like we're getting any older
But the memories build up around the eyes
And I need more fingers to count the ones I love
This life may be too good to survive

—Shovels & Rope, "St. Anne's Parade"

A few years after my bike trip, I got word from North Carolina that Brigitte had died from complications of what should have been routine heart surgery. Losing her was devastating and shocking. She was only sixty-three and had been a great athlete. She was far too young and healthy to be gone. The pain that stayed with me for many months was a sense that I had taken her friendship for granted, that Brigitte might have died not knowing how much she meant to me.

We packed a lot into our decade or so of friendship. She and I had connected over shared activities—yoga, running, biking, dogs, raising kids. She'd become a dear friend of Bob's as well, as a rabid sports fan and one who spoke her mind easily. It was a time of transition—we both became empty nesters, and Brigitte became a grandmother soon after I met her.

Bob and I kept moving further away from Greensboro and Brigitte, first to Durham, then the river house on the coast, then Rhode Island. We had fun visits and trips together after we left Greensboro, but it wasn't the same as playing together a few times a week and dropping by each other's houses. At one point, a few months before Brigitte died, I tried to tell her by phone from Rhode Island how much I missed her and how special her friendship was. "Oh honey, you have so many friends, all over the place!" she told me, brushing off my attempt to go deep.

Brigitte's parents came to the U.S. from France as young adults. I credit French culture for how she greeted friends with a hug and kiss, which seemed a bit physical to me. Very soon in our friendship she started ending our phone calls with "love you," which startled me at first. Slowly I began repeating it back to her. I did love Brigitte, but I wasn't practiced at telling anyone other than Bob—or maybe even Bob—that I loved them.

In Brigitte's honor, I have tried to change my ways, telling the people who are important to me that I love them. I am rich in friendships, which mean as much to me as ever. I treasure the friends I've known for decades and love that there's so much we don't have to explain to each other. But I'm also drawn to new friends, people who say yes to adventures big and small, who understand that it's time to seize the day. I want to do a better job of telling my friends how much they mean to me—while I still can.

Bob and I spent this past summer near Providence, Rhode Island, the closest I've lived to Dee since our early days in Boston. She and I got to play a lot—a few day-long bike rides, yoga classes, pickleball, and paddling kayaks. I feel a renewed appreciation for our friendship. I've taken time to examine what was going on with me on our bike trip, why I'd grown sensitive during all that intense time together. I had so much riding, excuse the pun, on the trip, such high expectations for it all that my sensors were on high alert.

Now I enjoy adding new miles to our friendship. One day last summer Dee and I biked from Providence to Westerly, the coastal Rhode Island town where Bob and I have lived a few times over the years. Dee planned the fifty-mile or so ride and a bus ride back home to Providence. At one point, making our way south on a back road on a summery morning, I did some quick math. "Dee! Do you realize we have been doing this for almost forty years?" I called up to her. It was funny to me, because at that moment I pretty much felt the same as I did in my twenties, pedaling along behind Dee, happy to be out playing on back roads on a nice morning.

These days when we say goodbye, I often hug Dee. Occasionally I tell her I love her.

Bob and Amos in our downsized townhouse in Durham, NC

LESSON 12

Downsize your stuff (the pannier effect).

I have a notion that if you are going to be spiritually curious, you better not get cluttered up with too many material things.
—Mary Oliver

What you don't have, you don't need it now
—U2, "Beautiful Day"

I'd been home from the bike trip for a month. I was driving home from the river house after a few summery days there, just me and the dogs. I was thinking about Bob's off-hand comment when I asked, back sometime during my trip, what he thought of me cutting back on work sooner than later, freeing up my time for more adventures. "We'll just have to find a way to make up for the lost income," he had said. I played with the math of me cutting back a day or two of work. Math and fractions are always a good distraction on long runs, rides, and drives because it takes me a long time to figure out the numbers. Like, if I'm at mile 330 of a 700-mile drive, how far along am I, percentage wise?

I drove through the flat expanses of eastern North Carolina, heading west to Durham, and calculated our finances. I thought about the house down the street from us, brand-new construction that just sold for

$625,000. Such prices were unheard of in our neighborhood just a few years earlier. That meant our three-bedroom bungalow has probably appreciated enough that we could sell it, find a little place for half its price, pay off our mortgage and be house-payment free. Our mortgage payment and taxes equaled probably half my monthly take-home pay. Voila, I had found a solution.

It's not just our finances I was considering. I have obsessed over houses for three decades. In our nine years in Ohio, we moved three times thanks to me falling in love with houses. I loved our Durham house with its broad front porch and its hip, updated kitchen. We had sweet young neighbors all around us with little ones we watched grow from babies to kindergartners. But I had the distinct feeling since I'd been home from my bike trip that the house was too much. It was fairly modest at 1,800 square feet. But we barely used the lower floor, with the third bedroom, bath, and little den. My friend Charlie calls it the pannier effect, the result of living happily for two months out of two panniers. I loved the simplicity, the lightness of not having much stuff. When I got home I couldn't imagine why I had so many clothes in my closet and in my dresser. I wanted less stuff, more experiences. Less clutter, more clarity.

And once again I was building a dream scenario, assembling a life from a mental catalog of possibilities. We could sell our house and buy something smaller that requires little maintenance, a place that we could leave easily for a month each summer. Bob was mostly free in July, and I could work remotely or take time off. And we could dip our toes into what retirement or semi-retirement feels like.

I pitched my plan to Bob once it was fully baked in my head. He was skeptical at first, as always. He was intrigued by the idea of shedding our mortgage. But all of a sudden he told me how much he loved our house. After complaining through my trip about how un-friendly our newest neighbors were, he started chat-ting more with them. He complained for a few years about mowing our bumpy yard, but suddenly he said it really wasn't that bad. Can you spot which one of us seeks and thrives on change and which one prefers things to stay the same?

I entered full obsession mode, checking real estate listings several times a day. There wasn't much out there in the lower price range, so I spent even more time comparing and contrasting, raising the maxi-mum price of what we'd consider. One day at work I saw that an interesting townhouse—a two-story, two-bedroom in a historic brick building with three other units—had just dropped its price by $50,000. It was a great location, highly walkable, and there was a spacious front porch. I called for an appointment and biked over that afternoon.

It's real estate lore that buyers make up their minds in the first fifteen seconds of seeing a house. My first fifteen seconds at the townhouse included walking up the front steps and seeing an upside-down U-shaped bike rack that the owners installed on the porch. Covered parking! That nearly did it for me. I stepped inside to discover a charming home, one of those rare cases where the rooms were bigger and better connected than the listing photos suggested. Bob took a look the next day and surprised me by liking the place. It felt more like city living, just a few blocks from Durham's Main Street. And it felt like coming full circle to our small apartment days in Boston. We made an offer the next day.

I spent the late summer and fall managing it all. I was a whirling dervish of energy. After work and weekends, I arranged to get our new place painted and repairs made at our current house. I hauled away carloads of our extra stuff to Goodwill. I made a few key purchases, upgrades: a memory foam mattress, a leather couch that doesn't hold dog fur. I lugged carloads of little stuff over to the new place for weeks so that on the day the movers brought our furniture, we were fully moved in. We hired a realtor to sell our place. He had a stager bring in hip furniture and accessories. Tommy said it looked like the Jetsons lived there. The house sold in a week for our asking price.

Josh was one of the neighbors I would miss the most in our neighborhood. He and his wife, Nola, lived next door and kept tabs on our plans, worrying about who would buy our place. He told me he wasn't surprised at all by our decision to move.

"I knew you would make some change after your bike trip," he told me. "You'd move, or maybe quit your job." To me, it was an exciting, surprising whirlwind of change and possibilities. I was kind of pinching myself that it was all happening, giddy with the new possibilities of financial freedom and downsized home ownership. But Josh saw it all coming. Was it that obvious?

As I was packing for our move, I came across a small, cloth-covered journal that I made for myself as I was graduating from high school. I worked that summer as a camp counselor on Cape Cod. My journal entries reflected the rollercoaster that was so much of my teens and early twenties. I was living and working in a beautiful place and teaching sailing. I had made friends with a few fellow counselors. When we shared the same days off, they would drive me to spend the day playing at the beach, staying through sunsets, often with a bottle of wine. On other days off I'd ride my bike out of camp and explore by myself. I was lonely, clearly, with my usual unrequited crushes and general lack of confidence. I didn't think I knew enough to teach sailing, I was a little scared to lead the campers, and I was sure I wasn't interesting enough for people to like me. I was nervous, too, about going to college. I made lists of things I wanted to buy to bring to school: LL Bean chamois shirts, a groovy Indian bedspread, a certain kind of coffee mug. My eighteen-year-old self believed that things—the right, curated things—would make me happy and would also help me find my soulmate.

Four decades later, I wanted to sit down with that younger self and tell her it's going to be OK. She will find dear friends and love. She will be lucky enough to raise two kids and share her values with them while they grow into their own interesting, confident selves. I'd tell her that sunsets and sunrises will continue to thrill her, just as nice meals or glasses of wine with friends still do. Certainly she'll have mind-numbing days of routine, days of hugging the shoulders of life's busy highway and hoping the thundering trucks and cars will stay in their lanes. She will need to cross big bridges, some of them scary—navigating her parents' last years of illness, say, and trying to launch a freelance business in a recession. But there will be days of sheer joy when the sun sparkles, the breeze is cool and smells of saltwater, her body flies along, and dear friends laugh with her. Mostly I would tell her to keep dreaming, because those dreams will guide her. The roads she chooses will take her exactly where she needs to go.

Living the dream: In the rain and mud in Maine on our second to last day

POSTSCRIPT

Chase your dreams.

One day you will wake up and there won't be
any more time to do the things you've
always wanted. Do it now.
—Paulo Coelho

Just a few days into our bike trip I started to recognize a certain familiar wistfulness as we'd tell someone what we were doing. Just south of Amelia Island in Florida, we stopped to chat with a park ranger on Little Talbot Island. He offered a few pointers, like where to pick up the greenway again on Big Talbot Island, just off a parking lot. When we told him that we were headed for the Canadian border, he looked off at the horizon. "I wish I could go with you," he said, not entirely joking.

Thousands of miles later, Mary, our host in South Dartmouth, Massachusetts, was heading out for a morning run as we packed up to leave her house. "Next trip, let me know," she told me, with the same wistful look on her face.

And Mark, watching us get our bikes ready in his yard to head out for our last week, said he felt suddenly jealous. After biking with us for four days he got it. Packing up each morning and heading out starts to feel like a way of life, knowing you'll encounter new places and people, sights and sounds, challenges and delights.

I recognized all of that wistfulness because I'd felt it most of my life. Ever since I was a young teen pining to live on a sailboat in the Fijis rather than be stuck in suburban Baltimore, restlessness and wanderlust have swum around in my subconscious. But I always thought adventures were what other people experienced, not me. Pick your excuse: I don't have the money, can't take the time off work, have to take care of the kids, can't leave Bob or the dogs, I don't know how, I'm a little scared.

Sensing the freedom of my third act is one of the lasting gifts of my bike trip. Having realized a dream—mapping it out, taking the journey, and reaping the benefits—I grow nearly evangelistic if someone tells me there's something they've always wanted to do. Especially if they are empty nesters with new-found time. Do it! Take the trip, take up the new sport, buy the getaway house, get rid of your stuff!

Bob retired a few years ago at sixty-seven. I work half-time at a good job that pays me well and gives me luxurious four-day weekends to play. Two years ago I biked from Pittsburgh to Washington, DC, with a friend, Jen, while Bob taught a class in England. This past fall I biked for three weeks from France to Germany with Jan, a friend I met in North Carolina. Bob met me in Germany and we biked for a week along the Danube River to Vienna.

If someone told me ten years ago that I would love my sixties this much, I might have laughed. I didn't know that yes, I'd be slower at sixty-three than fifty-three, but actually stronger because I have more time to be active. Mostly I hadn't yet learned how to drop all my excuses, all the reasons why I couldn't pursue dreams, and instead consider how I could. I am not reckless. I still meet my work deadlines and I don't burn cash in great big bonfires. But I am quicker to recognize possibilities and know when to say yes.

It's OK that I had to wait until my early sixties to get here. I feel rich in time, experience, and perspective. I've shushed my inner critic, for the most part, and in its place I hear all new compassion for myself and for others. I've done the work, I know I can carry myself over hills and across bridges. I'm even learning to recognize when it's OK to coast, when I can stop pedaling so hard because the wheels are spinning just fine.

Acknowledgements

Tyler Kober at Bullseye Bicycle in Durham, NC, helped ready my Kona Rove before I left town, even agreeing to add the woven-look grip tape I found for some bling. He has shared the story of our trip enthusiastically ever since we returned.

I'm indebted to my former East Coast Greenway Alliance co-workers: my boss Dennis Markatos-Soriano, first for giving me a great job and then for letting me leave for two months to ride my bike; Niles Barnes for patient assistance and suggestions on everything from navigation to gear to permission to ride the train into New York City; and Debbie West for listening to my stories, warning me against the Every Damn Inch club, and cheering me on.

Dee and I are much obliged to all the friends and family members who hosted us, fed us, met us, and led us over two months: Sherry Yonge, Delores Walters, Virginia DeRoy (Florida and New York City!), Terry Landreth, Brent Buice, Ron and Adrienne Watts, Kinga Rapacz, Dave Connelly, Kayla Craddock, Deb Lowry, Cindy Davis, Jane Wadsworth, Silvia Ascarelli and

Clive Jenner, Daniel Paschall and Korin Tangtrakul, Jeff Behm, Lou Rubin, Rob Dexter, Barbara Amodio, Beverly Duncan, Donna Koenig, Sarah Hreha, M'lyn Hines, Poyee Oster, Mary and Peter Kavanaugh, Donna Quirk, Bob Spiegelman, Mark and Laurie Neylon, Andy McClurg, Arnold Nadler, Al Nierenberg, Tom Gill, Barbara Pries, Becki Darling and Brad Minter, Dick Woodbury, Lauren Farkash, Diane Hessler—and so many more.

The friends and family who volunteered to stay at the river and watch Amos and Juno in weekly rotations are among my heroes. Sorry about the early mornings and any and all food that Amos helped himself to! Thank you Marylou LaLonde and Nancy Lilburn, Mary Loftus, Doris Beattie, Craig Himmelberger, Kate Malekoff, Melissa Doty, Sharon Gray, Erin and Noah Etheridge and family, and Adrienne Watts.

Silvia Ascarelli is a tireless advocate and friend. She not only hosted and biked with us (and bought our train tickets to New York City so we'd escape twenty or so hairy New Jersey miles), she also volunteered Jeff as a valuable guide north out of Manhattan and connected me with authors who could read near-final drafts of this book.

I am grateful to two wise editors, Elizabeth Bruno and Katie Bannon, who pushed me to tell the emotional story beneath the travelogue of this trip.

Talk about heroes: Sally Ann Hay drove Dee all the way from Providence, picked me up in North Carolina, and dropped us off in Key West, then drove all the way home by herself. Two months later she picked us up in Maine and drove us back to Providence. Which means Sally has singlehandedly driven the entire East Coast Greenway! She shared my nightly blog posts on her social media and carefully copy edited earlier versions of this story.

Ms. Bird, thanks for letting me sit beside you on the bus to the NU staff orientation oh so many years ago and all the adventures, inspiration, laughs, and lessons that have followed.

Dr. Malekoff, for decades you have been my first reader. I've asked you to tell me if an article I wrote for work made sense and if it was interesting. When I write something personal like a blog post, you always joke that you just skim the paragraphs looking for your name. So here it is: Love you, Bob.

Printed in the USA
CPSIA information can be obtained
at www.ICGtesting.com
LVHW010725060324
773528LV00007B/273